Social Studies
SKILLS
A WORKBOOK FOR HOMEWORK AND REVISION

RUTH NAUMANN

NELSON
A Cengage Company

Australia • Brazil • Japan • Korea • Mexico • Singapore • Spain • United Kingdom • United States

Social Studies Skills Book 1
1st Edition
 Ruth Naumann

Cover designer: Cheryl Rowe, Macarn Design
Text designer: Cheryl Rowe, Macarn Design
Production controller: Siew Han Ong

Any URLs contained in this publication were checked for currency during the production process. Note, however, that the publisher cannot vouch for the ongoing currency of URLs.

Acknowledgements
The author and publishers wish to thank the following:
For photographs:
Shutterstock, cover and pages 4, 6, 11, 12, 13, 14, 15, 22, 26, 27, 30, 31, 34, 36, 42, 45, 60, 63, 69, 70; Mark Elstone, page 21; Fairtrade, page 41; GeoEye, page 23; GNS Science, page 65; Alexander Turnbull Library, page 71, King, Marcus, 1891-1983 :[The signing of the Treaty of Waitangi, February 6th, 1840]. 1938; NZ Herald, page 8, 20
For cartoons:
Jim Hubbard, page 24; Robert Brockie, page 25

For product information and technology assistance,
in Australia call **1300 790 853**;
in New Zealand call **0800 449 725**

For permission to use material from this text or product, please email **aust.permissions@cengage.com**

National Library of New Zealand Cataloguing-in-Publication Data
National Library of New Zealand Cataloguing-in-Publication Data

Naumann, Ruth.
Social studies skills : workbook for homework and revision / Ruth Naumann.
(New Zealand basics)
ISBN 978-017023-076-6
1. Social sciences—Problems, exercises, etc.— Juvenile literature. [1. Social sciences—Problems, exercises, etc.] I. Title.
II. Series.
300.76—dc 23

Cengage Learning Australia
Level 7, 80 Dorcas Street
South Melbourne, Victoria Australia 3205

Cengage Learning New Zealand
Unit 4B Rosedale Office Park
331 Rosedale Road, Albany, North Shore 0632, NZ

For learning solutions, visit **cengage.com.au**

Printed in Malaysia by Papercraft.
16 17 25 24

Contents

1 Understanding Kiwiana

Think about identity, culture and organisation: how people pass on and sustain (keep going) culture and heritage and how this has results for people.

Generations of New Zealanders have formed a collection of things that are associated more closely with New Zealand than with any other country. This collection is often referred to as **Kiwiana**, *ana* meaning a collection. Kiwiana provides a sense of belonging and reminds people they are Kiwis, makes them recognisable to foreigners when they travel overseas, gives them a sense of security, encourages them to take pride in their country and helps them feel special. Kiwis regard Kiwiana as national treasure, as taonga, and pass this regard on to following generations as part of New Zealand culture – the set of beliefs and ways of behaviour Kiwis share.

Practice 1

The chart below has descriptions of 30 items of Kiwiana. The box under the descriptions contains the names of the items. Put the names of the items on the chart.

Skill: Responding to information in charts
- A **chart** is usually a summary of a large amount of information and so think about what may have been left out.
- When matching, do items you know first. Then come back to the others. This is called *a process of elimination*.
- Read descriptions carefully. They might include a word that is also in the name of the item.

Afghan	All Blacks	black singlet	Buzzy Bee
chocolate fish	fish and chips	gumboots	Edmonds Cookbook
Four Square	hangi	hei-tiki	hokey pokey icecream
jandals	kiwi	kiwifruit	Lemon and Paeroa
Marmite	national anthem	number 8 wire	paua shell
pavlova	peanut slab	Phar Lap	pineapple lumps
pohutukawa	silver fern	swanndri	Wattie's tomato sauce
	weetbix	whitebait fritters	

Frozen sweet with honeycomb toffee.	Biscuit topped with chocolate icing and a walnut.	Waterproof woollen and often tartan jacket.	Tree native to NZ.	Grocery store established in the 1920s.
Small fish caught in rivers and cooked in batter.	Breakfast cereal biscuit.	Used for sausage sizzle.	By-product of beer-brewing, used as food.	Soft drink with mineral water from North Island town.
Popular takeaway wrapped in newspaper.	Sleeveless, warm garment that does not show the dirt.	Waterproof rubber boots.	National rugby team.	Marshmallow candy.
Underground oven.	Flip-flops or thongs.	Song in Maori and English.	Nocturnal (out at night), flightless bird.	Christmas tree.
Chocolate-covered sweets with chewy insides.	Famous race-horse.	Chinese gooseberry.	Bright red and yellow clicking toy.	Meringue sweet with whipped cream and fruit.
Put out by makers of 'sure to rise' baking powder.	It is said Kiwis can fix or make anything with this.	Maori neck pendant.	Chocolate and nut bar.	Used for jewellery and decoration.

Practice 2

Choose an item of Kiwiana. It may be an item that is not one of the 30 mentioned in this unit. Then do the following activities.

Skill: Arguing a case clearly
- **Describe** means to give details about what something is like.
- **Explain** means to make clear, to make plain, to make understandable.
- If you choose an item you know well you can use your own knowledge without needing to research the item.

1 The name of your item is _____

2 Describe the item in your own words. _____

3 Explain how you have got to know it. _____

4 Explain why it has become part of Kiwi culture. _____
_____
_____

5 Explain how and why regard for the item will be passed on to the next generation.
_____
_____

ISBN: 9780170230766

2 Understanding culture

Think about identity, culture and organisation: how cultural interaction impacts on cultures and societies.

Culture means the ways of living that a group of people have built up and passed on from one generation to another. For example, when Maori and early Europeans made contact in New Zealand they found their two cultures had many differences such as language, houses, land ownership, food, gods, art, technology, and money. An important difference was how they passed their cultures down the generations. Europeans had a written culture because they read and wrote. Maori had an oral culture because they recorded memories using the spoken word.

Practice 1

Skill: Identifying items and practices
- **Identify** means to recognise or to show.
- An item is an article or a thing.
- A practice is an activity or a way of behaving.

Look at the images below and answer the questions that follow.

1 Identify by number the cultural item or practice most associated with

    a youth in New Zealand _____   **b** Maori _____   **c** Spain _____

    d Australia _____   **e** England _____   **f** India _____

    g Papua New Guinea _____   **h** Mongolia _____   **i** Japan _____

    j North American Indian _____   **k** Easter Island _____   **l** Zulus _____

2 Name three cultural practices least likely to be seen in New Zealand.

    a _____

    b _____

    c _____

ISBN: 9780170230766

3 Name the cultural item most likely to be the following.

   a Traditionally Asian but now consumed also by non-Asians in New Zealand.

_____

   b Traditionally used by nomads who move from place to place.

_____

   c Long-standing and mysterious feature on the landscape.

_____

4 Give a meaning for the following.

   a cultural practice _____

_____

   b cultural item _____

_____

Practice 2

Read the text below and then underline the actions taken to get biculturism in New Zealand.

Skill: Interpreting actions and ideas
- Ask the question, Did that action or idea aim to encourage biculturalism? (Example: Did the idea that Maori culture should adopt European culture aim to encourage biculturalism? No, it aimed to have one culture, not two.)
- Make sure you understand key terms. (Example: **Tangata Whenua** = Maori, **Tangata Tiriti** = non-Maori, originally Europeans who got the right to live in New Zealand from the Treaty of Waitangi.)

A word to do with culture is biculturalism. It is about having two important and equal cultures within a place or country. It appeared in New Zealand in the late 20th century and contained the idea that New Zealanders could be one country but have two peoples with their own cultures – Maori and European. Up till then the idea was that the minority Maori culture should adopt the majority European culture. Now the idea was that Maori could practise their own culture such as talking te reo, have their own education places such as kohanga reo, and run their own businesses, all of which would help Maori have more political and economic power. Treaty settlements to Maori gave them a financial base. Maori became an official language of New Zealand and many institutions such as government departments added Maori versions to their names. Te Papa in Wellington talked of its framework being based around the bicultural partnership between Tangata Whenua and Tangata Tiriti and the two different ways of seeing the world.

The Waitangi Tribunal was set up to make recommendations to Government on claims brought by Maori relating to Crown breaches of promises made in the Treaty of Waitangi. Some schools introduced bilingual units and classes. Kura Kaupapa Maori (Maori language immersion schools) were established and Maori were encouraged to become teachers.

ISBN: 9780170230766

3 Understanding multiculturalism

Think about identity, culture, and organisation: how cultural interaction has impacts on cultures and societies.

Multiculturism, sometimes called **diversity**, is 'multi cultures', more than two cultures. When a government talks of looking after multiculturism it means it wants all cultures and their practices to be respected. When waves of new settlers began to arrive in New Zealand from the Pacific Islands, Asia, Africa and the Middle East, people began to talk of multiculturalism. The term **ethnic group** is used to describe people who share a culture.

Practice 1

Study the chart showing the percentages of main cultures in some countries and answer the questions that follow.

Skill: Responding to information in percentages
- The figures after the ethnic groups are the percentages.
- Check information in brackets as it will be an explanation, definition or alternative term.
- Is there any ethnic group that is 100 percent of the population? Imagine how a mix of ethnic groups affects a country.

NEW ZEALAND: NZ European 74.5, Maori 9.7, Asian and others 7.4, Other European 4.6, Pacific Islander 3.8	BRAZIL: White 53.7, Mulatto (mixed White & Black) 38.5, Black 6.2, Other 0.9, Unspecified 0.7
RUSSIA: Russian 79.8, Tatar 3.8, Ukrainian 2.0, Bashkir 1.2, Chuvash 1.1, Other 12.1	MALAYSIA: Malay 60, Chinese 25, Indian 10, Other 5
JAPAN: Japanese 98.5, Korean 0.5, Chinese 0.4, Other 0.6	SINGAPORE: Chinese 76.8, Indian 7.9, Malay 13.9, Other 1.4
FIJI: Fijian 57.3, Indian 37.6, Rotuman 1.2, Other 3.9	AUSTRALIA: White 92.0, Asian 7.0, Aboriginal & Other 1.0
INDIA: Indo-Aryan 72, Davidian 25, Mongoloid and Other 3	QATAR: Arab 40, Indian 18, Pakistani 18, Iranian 10, Other 14
MYANMAR (BURMA): Burman 68, Shan 9, Karen 7, Rakhine 4, Chinese 3, Mon 2, Indian 2, Other 5	SOUTH AFRICA: Black 79.4, Coloured 8.8, White 9.2, Asian 2.6
CAMBODIA: Khmer 90, Vietnamese 5, Chinese 1, Other 4	MONACO: French 47, Monegasque 16, Italian 16, Other 21
SWITZERLAND: German 65, French 18, Italian 10, Romansch 1, Other 6	NAURU: Nauruan 58, other Pacific Islander 26, Chinese 8, European 8
TUVALU: Polynesian 96, Micronesian 4	THAILAND: Thai 75, Chinese 14, Other 11
SWAZILAND: African 97, European 3	SAUDI ARABIA: Arab 90, Afro-Asian 10
RWANDA: Hutu 84, Tutsi 15, Twa (Pygmy) 1	TURKEY: Turkish 80, Kurdish 20
SOMALIA: Somali 85, Bantu and other non-Somali 15	

ISBN: 9780170230766

1 How many ethnic groups are named in your country? _____

2 What is the majority one? _____

3 To which ethnic group do you belong? _____

4 What is the total of all the percentages in each box? _____

5 How are the percentages arranged? (Example: alphabetical order?)

_____

6 Which term includes ethnic groups that are not named? _____

7 Which term represents people who did not state their ethnic group? _____

8 In which country is the ethnic group that has the highest percentage?

_____

9 Which word shows that not every ethnic group is named? _____

10 Which country has a majority Black ethnic group? _____

11 Which two countries have the most similar ethnic groups? _____

12 In which country would Romansch be an official language? _____

13 Which countries have Arab as the main ethnic group? _____

14 In which ethnic group would Chinese in Fiji be classified? _____

15 In how many countries is Chinese named as an ethnic group? _____

16 In how many countries is Indian named as an ethnic group? _____

17 Which countries have ethnic groups similar to the names of the countries?

_____

18 In which country would conflict between Hutu and Tutsi happen? _____

19 What is a Mulatto? _____

20 What word is most likely to mean a native of Monaco? _____

Practice 2

Study the definition and example of a pie chart and do the activities below.

Skill: Using pie charts

- One way the percentages of ethnic groups can be shown is a pie chart (aka pie graph, circle graph). It is a circle divided into sectors or slices to show the relative sizes of each percentage.
- It is most useful for when there are only a few ethnic groups or when percentages are all between 25 – 50.
- Imagine how huge a pie chart would be needed to show percentages less than about 3.

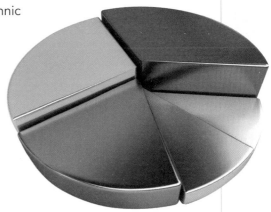

1 Highlight with one colour the five countries in the table on page 8 whose ethnic groups could be the easiest to show on a pie chart.

2 Highlight with another colour the ten countries in the table on page 8 whose ethnic groups could be the most difficult to show on a pie chart.

ISBN: 9780170230766

4 Understanding natural and cultural features

Think about place and environment: how exploration and innovation make chances and challenges for people, places and environments.

Just as your face has features such as eyes and ears, every place or environment has features. There are two types – natural and cultural. **Natural features**, such as mountains and rivers, are sometimes called physical features and are made by nature. They were present before people came to explore and they act as chances and challenges for people who have to work out how to live with them. **Cultural features**, such as railways and towns, are made by people and show how humans have impacted on places and environments as they change them in order to use them.

Practice 1

In the following chart highlight natural features with one colour and cultural features with another colour.

Skill: Sorting into categories
- When sorting, choose a key question to ask; for example, Was the feature made by nature or by people?
- Sometimes the answer is not immediately clear; for example, agricultural crops are cultural features because, even though plants are natural, people planted them deliberately. A zoo is a cultural feature, even though it is made up of natural vegetation and wild animals, because people made it.
- Think about how your environment is made up of natural and cultural features.

oil refinery	valley	park	town	igloo
village	church	ocean	river	canyon
mountain	foothills	railway	canal	quicksand
geyser	museum	orchard	tunnel	island
shelter belt	trig station	hot spring	wharf	zoo
gold mine	cemetery	pa	mangroves	vineyard
cableway	bridge	level crossing	sandy beach	maize crop
boat ramp	stopbank	motorway	creek	stone wall
stream	mudpool	cliff	hill	salt lake
cove	atoll	waterfall	brook	strait
scree	cave	lighthouse	industrial complex	tributary
native forest	market garden	fiord	desert	reservoir
peninsula	volcano	ridge	plain	mussel farm
palace	cathedral	polar cap	jetty	sea
dam	coral reef	sand dune	wind farm	castle
glacier	car-park	delta	estuary	ice shelf
barbary hedge	plateau	kiwifruit orchard	gulf	blowhole

ISBN: 9780170230766

Practice 2

For each of the following photographs give a natural feature, a cultural feature, a cultural practice, a likely place or environment it was taken.

a _____
b _____
c _____
d _____

a _____
b _____
c _____
d _____

a _____
b _____
c _____
d _____

a _____
b _____
c _____
d _____

a _____
b _____
c _____
d _____

a _____
b _____
c _____
d _____

ISBN: 9780170230766

5 Understanding consumer rights and responsibilities

Think about the economic world: how producers and consumers exercise their rights and meet their responsibilities.

All your life you will be a **consumer**, a person who uses goods and services produced in the economy. For example, you consume food by eating it, you consume power by watching television, you consume mobile phones by buying them and using them. If you get a job you will become a **producer** – someone who supplies goods and/or services in the economy. As a consumer you have rights and responsibilities. **Rights** are *permissions* given to you. For example, you have the right to not buy a pair of shoes even though the shop assistant has shown you 20 pairs. **Responsibilities** are your *obligations and duties* to act in certain ways. For example, you have the responsibility to take care with shoes you are trying on in a shop.

Consumer

Producer

Practice 1

The following chart contains some rights and responsibilities. Colour the rights one colour and the responsibilities another colour.

Skill: Examining and deciding
- **Examine** means to check carefully. Examine each item on the chart to decide if it is a right or a responsibility.
- To examine if it is a right, ask if it is something given to you. To examine if it is a responsibility, ask if it requires you to act in a particular way.
- Make sure you understand key terms; for example, **goods** = products such as food and clothing that satisfy human needs and wants, **services** = work done for others such as doctoring, educating, transporting.
- Imagine how your life would be different if you lived in a society without consumer rights and responsibilities.

Access to goods and services such as food and doctors.	Report wrong-doing and fraud to authorities.	Speak up if you feel you have been wronged.	Keep receipts, guarantees and contracts.
Legally buy and obtain goods and services.	A safe environment to live and work in.	Use a product for what it was intended.	A healthy environment to live and work in.
Realise you can't change your mind after you have bought and used a product.	Access to public utilities (services such as electricity and telephone).	Fair settlement of just claims such as compensation for shoddy goods.	Representation in the making and carrying out of government policy on consumer interests.
Check qualifications of service providers.	Avoid knowingly spreading disease.	Read contracts before signing.	Choice from a range of goods and services.

ISBN: 9780170230766

Make a good-faith effort to meet financial obligations.	Read and follow instructions on goods you buy.	Understand the environmental results of your consumption.	Protection against dangerous goods and services.
Choice of goods and services offered at competitive prices.	Check product at shop before buying or when it is delivered to you.	Research and compare goods and services before you buy.	Education about knowledge and skills needed to make informed choices about goods and services.

Practice 2

Each of the following ten actions shows a person being an irresponsible consumer. Beside each, put the action required for the person to be a responsible consumer.

Skill: Creative thinking
- Work out why the person was not being responsible; for example, if all tourists acted like Mia (below) they would harm the Tongan environment. If Mia was a responsible consumer, she should have enjoyed seeing coral in Tonga and brought home only photos of it.
- Refer back to the chart of rights and responsibilities.

1 Mia smuggled some coral home from her trip to Tonga. _____

2 Toby stole an iPod. _____

3 Paige complained to her mates but not to the shop that sold her a faulty DVD. _____

4 Angus broke his tennis racquet by using it as a hammer. _____

5 Lucia washed a jacket that was labelled Dry Clean Only. _____

6 Marcus threw away the guarantee for his new iPad. _____

7 Kayla wore her new boots to a dance before she decided she wanted to change them. _____

8 Seth failed to check a microwave when it was delivered to his home. _____

9 Pippa went shopping for a jacket and bought one in the first store she went to only to find the same jacket was much cheaper in another store. _____

10 Max bought a faulty video game from a street seller who wasn't there the next day. _____

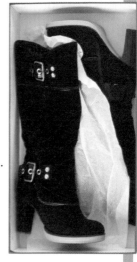

ISBN: 9780170230766

6 Understanding archaeology

Think about identity, culture and organisation: how people remember and record the past in different ways.

Archaeology is the **excavation** (digging up) of **sites** (places) and study of **artefacts** (man-made things) to find clues about how people lived in the past.

New Zealand has archaeological sites such as Maori pa and Maori and European middens (rubbish dumps). Archaeology has given information about ancient societies such as the Ancient Roman city of Pompeii and the Ancient Chinese Terracotta Army. The discovery in 1922 of the tomb of Tutankhamen, a pharaoh (emperor) in Ancient Egypt who came to power in 1333 BC at the age of nine or ten and died when he was about 18, produced his burial mask which is one of the most famous artefacts in the world.

Practice 1

Study the photo of archaeologists at work and then give six things about archaeology that would either encourage you to become an archaeologist who works on excavation sites or put you off becoming one.

Skill: Decision-Making
- To make an informed decision you need to gather as much information as you can, such as looking at the archeologists' age, fitness, tools, working conditions, clothing.
- Then think about what is not shown in the photo; for example, travel, discoveries in the soil, reactions from locals, recording the past.

1 _____
_____
2 _____
_____
3 _____
_____
4 _____
_____
5 _____
_____
6 _____
_____

ISBN: 9780170230766

Practice 2

Analyse the photo of the burial mask of Tutankhamun by answering the questions that follow.

1 For whom was the burial mask made?
_____

2 What part of the world does it come from?
_____

3 Where would it have been discovered?
_____

4 When was it discovered? _____

5 Why was it created? _____
_____

6 What was it used for?
_____
_____

7 Where would it have been placed in relation to the dead person? _____
_____

8 Why do you think it was made of gold?
_____

9 Why would some other burial masks be made of material that was painted to look like gold? _____

10 How was it made? (By machine?) _____

11 What does it suggest about the technology of the time? _____
_____

12 What are the two emblems on the forehead? _____
_____

13 What is on the chin of the mask's face? _____

14 Describe the collar. _____

15 Describe the makeup around the eyes. _____

16 What is the face wearing on its head? _____

17 What does it tell us about the life and times of the people who used it?
_____

18 Would New Zealanders use it today? Why, or why not? _____
_____

19 Why do you think it is thought to be so important? _____
_____

20 Would it have had any other uses? _____
_____

ISBN: 9780170230766

How to analyse line and column graphs

Think about the economic world: how economic decisions impact on people, communities and nations.

Graphs communicate information visually and help you understand data.

Study the line graph below and answer the questions about it.

Skill: Responding to a graph
- Vertical line = **y axis** (think 'y goes to the sky'), usually has measures of amounts increasing at regular intervals marked up it.
- Horizontal line = **x axis**, usually has measures of time increasing at regular intervals marked along it.
- A ruler gives accuracy when reading a graph; for example, to find the unemployment rate for 2000 put the ruler vertically on the mark for 2000 on the x axis, note where it meets the graph line, put the ruler horizontally on that place and you will see the ruler meets 6 on the y axis meaning the answer is 6 percent.

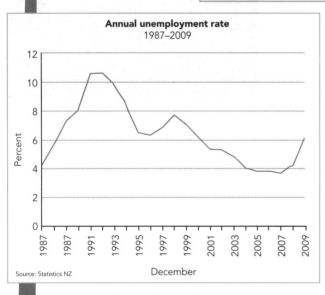

Annual unemployment rate
1987–2009

Percent

December

Source: Statistics NZ

1 What is the title of the graph?

2 Which word in the title means yearly?

3 Which word in the title means not having a job? _____

4 What time period does the graph show?

5 How many years are there on the graph?

6 Who created this graph?

7 How do you know this is about New Zealanders? _____

8 What is the name of the graph's vertical line? _____

9 What do the figures on this line measure? _____

10 What is the name of the graph's horizontal line? _____

11 What do the numbers on this line represent? _____

12 What shape do the vertical and horizontal lines make together? _____

13 Give one reason why you would call this graph a line graph.

14 'The x axis increases at regular intervals.' Is that statement true or false? Explain your answer. _____

15 'The y axis increases at regular intervals.' Is that statement true or false? Explain your answer. _____

ISBN: 9780170230766

16 Give a reason the percent figure stops at 12. _____

17 Which year had the lowest percent? _____

18 What was the percent in 1991? _____

19 Was the percent for 2004 higher or lower than that for 2009? _____

20 What was the difference in percent between 1990 and 2000? _____

Practice 2

Study the graph below and answer the questions about it.

Skill: Responding to a graph

- Data presented as horizontal bars make a **bar graph**; vertical bars make a **column graph**.
- In 1970 rich countries agreed to give 0.7 percent of their gross national income (all the money a country earns in a year) as official development assistance to developing countries each year. Since then, billions have been given but rarely have rich countries met their promised target.
- Use a ruler for accuracy; for example, to find out New Zealand's percentage put the ruler horizontally at the top of its bar and note where the ruler meets the y axis. You will see the answer is 0.3.

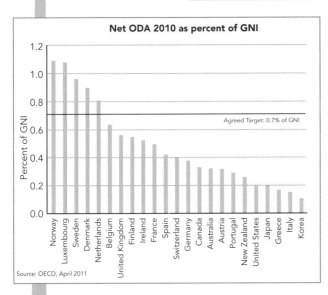

Net ODA 2010 as percent of GNI

Source: OECD, April 2011

1 What is the title of the graph?

_____

2 Who created the graph? _____

3 When was the graph published? _____

4 What is ODA?

_____

5 What is GNI?

_____

6 Is this graph a bar graph or a column graph? Give a reason for your answer.

_____

_____

7 What is shown on the x axis? _____

8 What is shown on the y axis? _____

9 Are the gaps between the bars all the same? _____

10 What is the range of measures on the y axis? _____

11 How many countries are named? _____

12 Suggest a reason there are only two Asian countries and no African countries.

_____

13 The US often gives the most money. How does it rank in terms of meeting its agreed target? _____

14 Which countries exceeded their targets? _____

15 Which countries did not meet their targets? _____

16 Which countries did not get halfway to their targets? _____

17 Where did New Zealand rank? _____

18 What percentage of its GNI did New Zealand donate? _____

19 What percentage of its GNI did Norway donate? _____

20 What percentage of its GNI did Australia donate? _____

ISBN: 9780170230766

How to analyse a map

Think about place and environment: how people move between places and how this has results for the people and the places.

A **map** is a picture, drawing or representation of the Earth's surface that shows how features such as a city and lake are related to each other by size, distance and location. There are many types of map. For example, a physical map shows features such as rivers. An economic or resource map shows the location of resources such as gold. A political map shows boundaries between regions or countries.

Practice 1

Study the map and answer the questions that follow.

Skill: Responding to a map
- Use tools on the map to help you such as compass rose (aka orientation) to show direction and location, scale to show distance, title to show the topic, key (aka legend) to show what symbols and/or colours mean, border (aka frame) to show edge of the mapped area.
- Three main horizontal lines show the equator, tropic of Cancer (north of equator), and tropic of Capricorn (south of equator).
- Use your background knowledge such as Cook was English, sailing ships were tiny, conditions on board were cramped with unwashed sailors and no modern technology, Cook's journals showed New Zealand would be suitable for British settlers, the courage of sailors.

Voyages of Captain Cook

N
↑

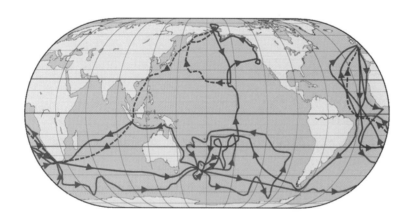

KEY
——— 1st voyage
——— 2nd voyage
——— 3rd voyage
- - - - crew after Cook's death

1 What is the title and how does it help you understand the map better?

_____

2 What evidence is there that Cook was a great explorer?

_____

3 What is the purpose of the arrow with N above it?

_____

4 Label the equator, tropic of Cancer and tropic of Capricorn lines.

ISBN: 9780170230766

5 Are these lines real or imaginary? Explain your answer. _____

_____

6 Name the country and continent from which Cook set sail on his voyages.

_____

7 In which direction did Cook head at the beginning of his voyages? _____

8 In which ocean was Cook killed? _____

9 What does the map show about Cook's relationship with Antarctica? _____

_____

10 What does the map show about Cook's relationship with the Great Barrier Reef?

_____

11 How would Cook's voyages have influenced people to settle in New Zealand?

_____

12 What effect would this have had on the people already living there? _____

_____

Practice 2

Study the map of Bora Bora, and, and answer the questions that follow.

Skill: Responding to a map
- Bora Bora is in French Polynesia and said by many to be the most stunning island in the world. It was formed after volcanic eruptions on the ocean floor caused lava to break through the ocean surface and has the remains of the volcano in its centre.
- Use your background knowledge; for example, **lagoon** = stretch of salt water separated from open sea, **coral** = marine organism that builds reefs in tropical oceans, **reef** = ridge just below or above the water surface.

Bora Bora
Tahiti Islands

Airport
REEF
Motu Tofari
Motu Tevairoa
REEF
Bora Bora
▲ Mt Otemanu
REEF
REEF
Motu Maoaohonuu
Motu Piti Aau
REEF
Matira Beach
REEF
REEF
PACIFIC OCEAN

1 In which ocean is the island located?

_____

2 Suggest a reason a scale is not given. _____

_____

_____

3 Describe the shape of the island. _____

_____

4 Give two ways you could get to this island. _____

_____

5 What word on the map describes small islands forming the reef? _____

6 Describe the location of the gap in the reef and the purpose it serves. _____

_____

7 The map features a lagoon. Label this on the map.

8 Explain why the lagoon is calm. _____

9 What is most likely to be the highest place on the island? _____

10 Do you think Bora Bora is an active or an extinct volcano? Give a reason for your answer.

_____

11 Suggest a reason it is a major international tourist destination. _____

_____

12 What effect would this have on the people living there? _____

_____

ISBN: 9780170230766

How to analyse a photo

Think about identity, culture and organisation: how people take part as individuals and in groups in response to community challenges; how people seek human rights.

An old saying goes 'A picture paints a thousand words.' A photo, short for photograph, is a picture recorded by a camera. It freezes a slice of life at a particular time and place. As such it is a powerful image, so powerful that there are still people who refuse to be photographed because they think photos steal their souls.

Practice 1

Study the photo about protest action and answer the questions that follow.

> **Skill: Responding to a photograph**
> - Use any background knowledge you have; for example, these students had been occupying a floor at the university in protest against increases in student fees and against a new law passed by the government.
> - Think about meaning (*What is it about?*), content (*What can I see?*), setting (*Where and when was it taken?*), purpose (*Is it a real event or was it staged?*), mood (*How does it make me feel?*)
> - Think about why people protest and its effects.

Auckland University protesters surround a police car.

1 In which country was the photo taken?
_____

2 Is the photo taken in a studio or outside?
_____

3 Give a detail to back up your choice.
_____

4 Where was the photographer standing?
_____

5 Does it show recognisable objects or is it taken at an unusual angle or with an unusual lens?
_____

6 Where is the caption (what the photo is about) placed? _____

7 What information does the caption give you? _____

8 Is there a focal point, a place where your eye keeps returning? If so, what is it?
_____

9 Which two groups of people are in the photo? _____

10 Which group wears a uniform? _____

11 Why is the other group in mufti? _____

12 What do the clothes suggest about the weather? _____

13 Which group were the protesters? _____

14 Suggest a reason there are no banners or signs. _____
_____

15 What one action are the students doing as a group? _____

ISBN: 9780170230766

16 What one action are the police doing as a group? _____

17 Is there any evidence of weapons? _____

18 If this photo was published in an overseas newspaper, what impressions about New Zealand society might a viewer get? _____
_____

19 Is the photo's main job to record an event, or is it concerned with communicating emotion and trying to get you to feel certain emotions? _____
_____

20 Does the photo raise any questions for you? If so, what? _____
_____

Practice 2

Study the photo of the stranded ship and fill out the chart that follows.

Skill: Responding to a photo

- Use any background knowledge you have; for example, in October 2011 this container ship, the *Rena*, hit the Astrolabe Reef about 12 nautical miles off Tauranga and began discharging oil, containers and rubbish into the sea and along the coastline.
- Study the photo for several minutes to get an overall idea of it and then look at individual items in it. Then divide the photo into quadrants (four sections) and look at each quadrant to see if new details come to light. Then study the photo again to see if there is anything you have missed.

People	Objects	Action/Activities
Light	**Setting**	**Colour**

New Zealand's worst marine environmental disaster.

Based on what you have listed above, give three comments you could make about this photo.

1 _____

2 _____

3 _____

Give two questions this photo has raised for you.

1 _____

2 _____

Give two places you might find answers to them.

1 _____

2 _____

ISBN: 9780170230766

10 How to analyse an aerial photo

Think about place and environment: how people view and use places differently.

Later on you will learn how to draw a sketch to summarise and simplify what you see in an aerial photograph. To get a heads up you can start thinking about aerial photographs now. There are two main types, depending on the angle the photographer uses. An **oblique aerial photo** means the photographer was looking down and across. A **vertical aerial photo** means the photographer was looking straight down.

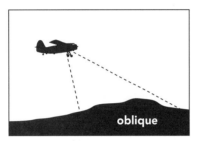
oblique

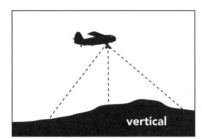
vertical

Practice 1

Study the photo of the rainforest and answer the questions that follow.

Skill: Responding to an oblique aerial photo
- Look for a title or a caption which will give you information.
- Generally, dark and rough patches with uneven patterns = native bush, forest, or jungle; light and smooth patches = cleared areas (deforestation); winding or straight ribbons = rivers; whitish or very bright patches = beaches.
- Imagine the different views on this place – environmentalists wanting to keep it as a wilderness and use the trees to help clean the air of toxic gases; developers wanting to build hotels; farmers wanting to clear it for farms.

1 In which country was the photo taken? _____

2 Name two things the photographer could have been travelling in.
_____

3 Explain why this is an oblique aerial photo. _____
_____

4 How would it be different if it was a vertical aerial photo?
_____

5 What is the main water feature? _____

6 Describe the shape of this feature. _____

7 What is the main type of vegetation? _____

8 How close is this vegetation to the main water feature?
_____

9 Is there any evidence of deforestation? If so, where?
_____

Aerial view of rainforest in Brazil.

ISBN: 9780170230766

10 Is there any evidence of development projects? If so, where? _____

11 Give a reason that the river looks navigable. _____

12 Sandbanks and 'beaches' appear in this area between May and October. During which months was this photo taken? _____

Practice 2

Study the photo of the Gemasolar Power Plant near Seville in southern Spain and answer the questions that follow.

> **Skill: Responding to a vertical aerial photo**
> - Use background knowledge. 185 hectares of plant consists of over 2,600 mirrored panels which reflect sunlight to a concrete solar tower 40 stories high which stores heat and converts it to energy making it the world's first solar power station that generates electricity at night.
> - Vertical photos can create optical illusions; for example some people say this photo looks like a human eye.
> - Man-made features such as buildings are generally of uniform shapes such as squares, rectangles, circles; and transport systems such as roads fairly straight ribbons often in grid patterns.

1 Why is it called a vertical aerial photo?

_____

2 How would it be different if it was an oblique aerial photo? _____

_____

3 Was it taken at night or during the day?

_____

4 Was it taken in a rural or urban area?

_____

5 Give a reason based on evidence in the photo for your answer to the previous question.

_____

_____

_____

6 Give a reason based on deduction (your logical thinking) for why the power plant is located in a rural or urban area. _____

_____

7 What pattern do the mirrored panels make? _____

8 The photo is said to have a Sc-fi movie look about it. Do you agree? Why or why not?

_____

_____

9 What man-made feature are the generally straight brown lines on either side of the power plant? _____

10 Name another man-made feature in the photo. _____

11 Where is the tower located? _____

12 Describe what the tower looks like in the photo. _____

_____

_____

ISBN: 9780170230766

How to analyse a cartoon

Think about continuity (past, present, future) and change: how people in different times and places respond differently to the Treaty of Waitangi.

A **cartoon** is a simple sketch drawn in a humorously exaggerated way about someone or something in the news. It is a popular feature in newspapers and some magazines.

Practice 1

Study the cartoon about Waitangi Day and write some notes beside the cartoon checklist that follows.

Skill: Interpreting a point of view
- **Interpret** means to explain the meaning of something.
- Think about what is obvious and not so obvious in the cartoon and the aim of the cartoonist.
- Use background knowledge; for example, the Treaty of Waitangi was signed on 6 February 1840 between the British Government and some Maori chiefs in Waitangi in NZ's Bay of Islands before it went around NZ for other chiefs to sign, and ever since people have had differing responses to it and to Waitangi Day.
- Make sure you understand key terms; for example, **agendas** = underlying aims and motives, **apathy** = lack of enthusiasm, **controversy** = disagreement, **humbug** = false, **torrential** = falling quickly and heavily. (There is a spelling mistake in the cartoon below – can you find it?)

Jim Hubbard, 5 February 2010.

Cartoon checklist

1 Date of publication? _____

2 Cartoonist? _____

3 Setting (where action takes place)? _____

4 Action? _____

5 Dress? _____

ISBN: 9780170230766

6 Date for forecast?_____

7 Name of special day _____

8 Map symbols (signs that stand for something)?_____

9 Five weather words and terms?_____

_____

10 One way the cartoon shows it is about NZ? _____

_____

11 Another way it shows this?_____

_____

12 And another way it shows this?_____

_____

Practice 2

Study the cartoon about Maori claims to the Waitangi Tribunal and make notes that you could use for a paragraph about the cartoon.

Skill: Interpreting a point of view

- Making your own notes is harder than having questions to answer. Use background knowledge; for example, today there is a Treaty Tribunal that listens to Maori claims against the Crown (the NZ Government).
- Make sure you understand key terms eg. gravy train = making a lot of money for little work.
- Think about what is obvious and not so obvious in the cartoon and the cartoonist's aim.
- Remember a cartoon is just one person's view about something. Another cartoonist or the same cartoonist living in a different time may have drawn a cartoon showing the positive aspects of the Treaty of Waitangi such as Maori having the chance to have their claims heard.

Robert Brockie, 12 September 2009.

ISBN: 9780170230766

How to analyse a poster

Think about continuity and change: how the ideas and actions of people in the past have had an important impact on people's lives.

Because posters are designed to be displayed in public they aim to be eye-catching so people will get the message. Cheap to make and easy to put up, they were used during World War 1 (1914-18) and World War 2 (1939-45) to spread propaganda which is information, especially one-sided or misleading, used to make people support something like a political party or a war. Hitler used posters to get people to follow his Nazi party, to believe Jews were enemies, and to see him as the Führer, leader of Germany.

Practice 1

Study the poster and answer the questions about it.

Skill: Interpreting a symbol
- A **symbol** is something that represents or stands for something else. The kiwi is a symbol of New Zealand. Here the man is Uncle Sam, a symbol of the U.S. Government.
- Think about the time period. This 1917 poster was used to recruit soldiers for World War I. The US entered World War 1 in April 1917, choosing up till then not to get involved in the problems of other countries.
- Think about what the poster shows and says, and why it was made.
- Imagine the effects of encouraging American people to support the war and how such effects have helped shape the world you live in today.

1 With which country is the poster associated? _____

2 When did the poster first appear? _____

3 What is the name of the person featured? _____

4 For what is this person a symbol? _____

5 How is he portrayed? (eg. young or old) _____

6 In what way is his clothing linked to a flag? _____

7 Why was the poster created? _____
_____

8 Give one way the poster tries to get your attention. _____
_____

9 Give another way the poster tries to get your attention. _____
_____

10 How does it try to make viewers feel important? _____
_____

ISBN: 9780170230766

11 What is a recruiting station? _____

_____

12 How does the last line reinforce the message of the first two lines? _____

_____

Practice 2

Study the Nazi posters and answer the questions about them.

> **Skill: Identifying propaganda**
> - Consider how posters were used as propaganda. The top Nazi Party poster is advertising a 1933 film called *SA Mann Brand* in which Herr (Mr) Brand acts as a hero all the time to show how wonderful Hitler's Storm Troopers (Sturmabteilung) are. The bottom poster advertises Hitler and the Nazi Party and uses the famous Nazi symbol of the swastika, the crooked cross.
> - Use background knowledge; for example, *Nazi* comes from **Na**tional So**zi**alstische Deutsche Arbeiterpartei - the National Socialist German Workers' party.
> - Imagine what might have happened if people had ignored such posters and refused to vote for Hitler and the Nazis.

1 With which country are the posters associated?

_____

2 Which political group are the posters about?

_____

3 Which group of people belonging to this political party is featured? _____

4 Who would have put the posters up?

_____

5 Suggest a reason the posters are free of graffiti.

_____

6 Which symbol is a feature of both posters?

_____

7 What does this symbol look like?

_____

8 What does Herr Brand look like? _____

9 Why would these posters appeal to people unable to read or write?

_____

10 How are they designed to catch your eye? _____

_____

11 What is the aim of both posters? _____

_____

12 Why could they be called propaganda? _____

_____

ISBN: 9780170230766

How to show location

Think about continuity and change: how events have causes and effects.

Location refers to a point on a surface such as Earth where a feature exists or an event took place. For example, when the earthquake of 22 February 2011 caused death and destruction in Christchurch, newspaper stories around the world included maps of New Zealand and of Christchurch to locate the places for readers.

Practice 1

Study the map and describe the location of Christchurch by answering the questions that follow.

Skill: Describing a location
- Being able to describe the location is an important part of understanding causes and effects of an event or describing a particular natural or cultural feature.
- When describing location, relate it to neighbouring features and places, such as an ocean.

1 In what ocean is Christchurch located?

_____

2 On what island is it located?

_____

3 Describe the location of this island in relation to the other islands shown.

_____

_____

4 In what region is Christchurch located?

_____

5 Name four regions you would mention when describing the location of this region.

_____

_____

6 Describe the location of Christchurch in relation to the country's capital city.

_____

_____

_____

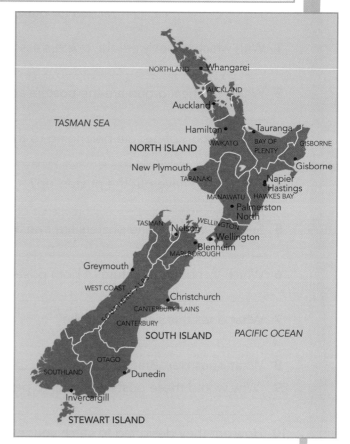

7 Name natural features you could mention when describing the location of Christchurch and the surrounding area. _____

_____

_____

ISBN: 9780170230766

8 In the first blank box practise sketching the South Island and marking in the location of Christchurch on your sketch. Then cover up your practice map and draw the same map from memory in the second box. Check your map and give it a mark out of three. Your mark =

| | |
| | |

Practice 2

Study the map of the location of Ancient Egypt and fill out the chart. Try to use a cardinal compass point for each location.

Skill: Using cardinal compass points

- Cardinal compass points are North, South, East, West and are useful for showing location; for example, Ancient Egypt was divided into two regions, known as Upper Egypt and Lower Egypt. Lower Egypt was in the north where the Nile fanned out with several mouths to form the Nile Delta. Upper Egypt in the south, stretched to what is now Aswan.
- Imagine the impact on modern lives that the people of ancient Egypt had; for example, their choice of where to locate their towns.

Place	Where the place was located
Valley of the Kings	
Lower Egypt	
Upper Egypt	
Red Sea	
Thebes (Luxor)	
Dahshur	
Cairo	
Giza	
Nile delta	
Aswan (Swenet)	

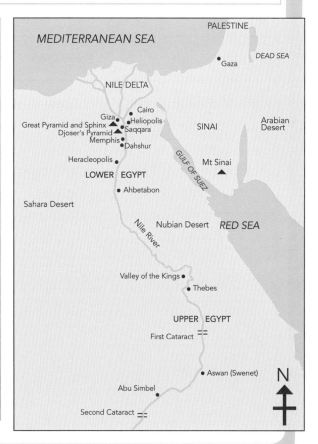

ISBN: 9780170230766

How to locate Asia

Think about place and environment: how people move between places and how this has results for the people and the places.

Because it is the closest and offers so many trading opportunities, the continent of Asia is becoming more and more important to New Zealand. There are many different opinions on which countries are considered part of Asia. The 33 countries named in this unit are the ones that are the most often listed as belonging to Asia or partly to Asia as is the case with Turkey and Russia.

Practice 1

Familiarise yourself with the names of the countries by underlining letters that could be spelling traps. For example, Philippines, Bhutan, Kyrgyzstan. Use the spare boxes to practise the spellings.

Skill: Familiarising
- To make things better-known you need to get familiar with them. You could colour-code the names into ones you know and ones you don't know, or use a tick and cross system. Learning the spellings will help make them more familiar.
- Notice alternative names. For example, Kampuchea is the local name for Cambodia.
- Think about why the movement of people between New Zealand and Asia makes it important for you to know about Asia.

Afghanistan	Bangladesh	Brunei	Bhutan
Cambodia/Kampuchea	China	India	Indonesia
Iran	Japan	Laos	Kazakhstan
Kyrgyzstan	Malaysia	Maldives	Myanmar/Burma
Nepal	Mongolia	North Korea	Pakistan
Philippines	Singapore	Sri Lanka	South Korea
Russia	Taiwan	Thailand	Timor-Leste/East Timor
Tajikistan	Turkey	Turkmenistan	Uzbekistan
Vietnam			

ISBN: 9780170230766

Practice 2

Write the names of the countries on the map to show their locations. The letters show you what the name of each country starts with. Colour countries different colours to distinquish them.

Skill: Recognising and placing

- Use what you know already eg. Korea used to be referred to as a dagger pointing at the heart of China; Myanmar, Thailand, Cambodia, Laos and Vietnam are on the Indochinese Peninsula; Taiwan is called the Republic of China; Mongolia is located between Russia and China; Japan, Philippines, Singapore, Indonesia, Sri Lanka, Brunei, Timor-Leste, Taiwan are island countries.
- Imagine if you were applying for a job and the interviewer asked you how you felt about flying to Indonesia once a month and you had no idea where Indonesia was. Do you think you would get the job?

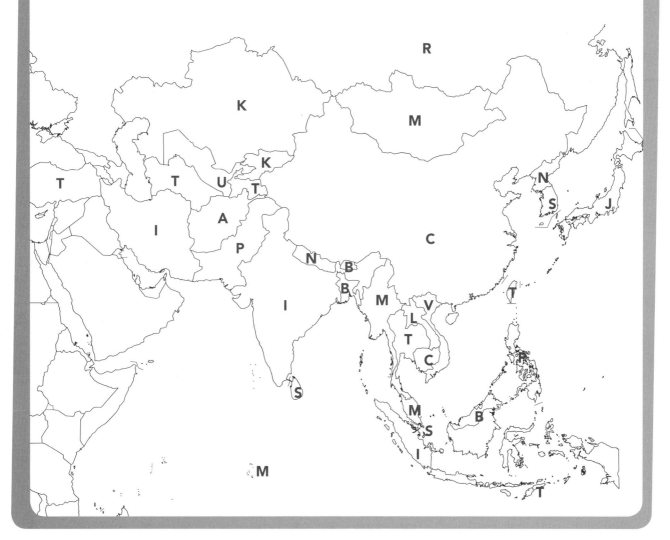

ISBN: 9780170230766

How to make a flow chart

Think about continuity and change: how events have causes and effects.

A flow chart shows the order in which steps happen during an event. It is often a row of boxes in vertical or horizontal order, with each box joined to the next with an arrow to indicate the direction to follow.

Practice 1

Study the text about earthquakes and highlight pieces that would be most useful for a flow chart about 'How Earthquakes Happen'.

Skill: Selecting
- To help you select pieces ask, does it answer the question 'How do earthquakes happen'? The first sentence is about a nickname and how many biggish earthquakes NZ has a year. Nothing in it helps answer the question, 'How do earthquakes happen?' and so nothing in it would be useful on a flow chart.
- Don't include meanings of terms and words on a flow chart. Use the term only; for example, 'tectonic plates', not 'tectonic plates which are the vast slabs of rock of Earth's surface'.

New Zealand, not called The Shaky Isles for nothing, has over 250 significant earthquakes each year. It is estimated that around the world each year there are 500,000 detectable earthquakes which strike suddenly and without warning. The sudden movement or shaking in the Earth's crust, known as an earthquake, begins with an event such as a meteor hitting Earth, a volcanic eruption, a nuclear explosion, a mine blast or, as is most common, movement of tectonic plates. These plates are the 20 or so vast slabs of rock that make up Earth's surface and slowly move and float on molten rock. New Zealand sits on the boundary between the Pacific Plate and the Indo-Australian Plate. At boundaries of the plates, plates can push against each other, slide by each other or brush against one another. This causes stress to build up in the upper, brittle layers of the plates. A fault line, a break in Earth's crust where blocks of crust are moving in different directions, forms. Most earthquakes happen along a fault line. The movement of the two plates makes the rock along the line more and more stressed. The plates get stuck together at their edges while the rest of the plate moves. The pressure keeps building until suddenly the plates unstick and set off an earthquake which releases energy as different types of waves. The waves we feel and that cause most damage as they move up and down the surface of Earth rocking foundations of man-made structures are surface waves. They are the slowest moving of all the waves which means they arrive last and why the worst shaking usually comes at the end of the earthquake. Once the ground has stopped shaking survivors are able to see the effects. For example, the February 2011 earthquake in Christchurch killed 181 people, damaged and destroyed buildings and water and sewerage systems, sent hundreds of thousands of tonnes of silt bubbling up from the ground, set off aftershocks and caused the Government to declare a state of national emergency.

ISBN: 9780170230766

Practice 2

Study the text about a volcanic eruption and fill in the flow chart to show the order in which steps happen.

Skill: Creating a visual
- Give your flow chart a title.
- Work out what the main steps are. Each main step goes in a separate box. Look for clue words such as first, begins, therefore, second, next, then, after, now, finally.
- Rewrite each step as a brief summary and add arrows.
- Imagine the fiery power deep within the Earth that produces the volcano.

What will be a volcanic eruption begins when great heat and pressure cause some of the mantle, the solid formation of rock inside Earth, to melt. This mantle is a vast part of Earth and can get to over 1,000 degrees Celsius. The melted rock is known as magma. It is lighter than the solid rock around it and therefore it rises and gathers below the Earth's crust (the top layer of Earth on which life exists) in a reservoir known as the magma chamber of a weak part of overlaying rock. When magma pressure rises and the magma has to get out somehow, or when a crack opens up in Earth's crust, out spews the magma, along with gases and other debris such as ash, through an opening called a vent or a fissure. The magma is now known as lava and it forms a volcano. The volcano's mountain-like mound is what remains after the material spewed during eruptions has collected and hardened around the vent. That could take a few weeks or many millions of years.

ISBN: 9780170230766

How to make a comic strip

Think about identity, culture and organisation; how formal and informal groups make decisions that impact on communities.

A comic strip is a sequence of drawings in boxes with text in captions and balloons. Creating a comic strip from text is a way of summarising main points. The story the comic strip tells can be funny (hence the name comic strip) or serious.

Practice 1

Read the text about Hillary's ascent of Everest and highlight what you would show in a comic strip.

Skill: Identifying essentials
- As a comic strip needs to look uncluttered identify only the most essential information to use. Search for people, places, heights, actions and events.
- Make sure you understand key terms; examples, **Himalayas** = mountain range in Asia between India, Pakistan, Nepal, Bhutan and China; **base camp** = where supplies are kept; **col** = pass between mountain peaks.
- Picture the decisions here and the far-reaching results of them.

In 1953 a British expedition, led by John Hunt and consisting of over 400 people including Kiwi Edmund Hillary and Tensing Norgay from Nepal, was in the Himalayas trying to become the first in the world to conquer Mount Everest, Earth's highest location. In March the expedition set up base camp and then at the South Col, 7,890 metres up, it set up the final camp. On May 26 a pair of climbers tried to get to the top

of Everest but had to turn back. Hunt then told Hillary and Norgay to try but high wind and snow kept them at the South Col until they set off on May 28. At 8,500 metres they put up their tent. Next morning Hillary's boots were frozen solid and he spent two hours defrosting them. He and Norgay then reached the last challenge – a 12 metre rock face. Hillary slid up a crack in the face and Tenzing followed him. At 11.30 a.m. they reached 8,849 metres, the summit of Everest. They hugged each other and Tenzing buried sweets and biscuits in the snow as a Buddhist offering to the gods while Hillary left a cross. Hillary took photos looking down the mountain to show they had reached the top and of Tenzing, but as Tenzing did not know how to use a camera there were no photos of Hillary. Because they were low on oxygen they stayed for only fifteen minutes but when they descended they found snow had already covered their tracks. The first person they met was George Lowe, another Kiwi, who had come up with hot soup. Seeing how exhausted the two men looked Lowe thought they had failed, until the two pointed to the mountain and signalled they had got to the top.

Practice 2

Read the following extract about an event in 19ᵗʰ century New Zealand and plan out a comic strip from it in the space provided.

Skill: Planning

- **Planning** means you just show what would go in each box.
- Decide how many boxes you will need. They can be different sizes.
- Work out a title and any captions (words to show things like location or time). Write captions in present tense; for example, *She races*.
- The tail of a speech balloon points to the speaker's mouth. The tail of a thought balloon (shown by several bubbles) points to the thinker's head.
- Sound effects can be one word; for example, SQUELCH.
- Concentrate on showing action rather than too much talk.
- Make sure you understand key terms; examples, **colonial oven** = cast-iron box with door that sat in a fireplace, **stalwarts** = strong and loyal, **coercion** = forcing, **cortege** = solemn procession, **apparition** = something that appears, especially if it is startling.
- Imagine all the decisions involved in this one event and their results.

"Oh, father!" I exclaimed in a sudden spasm of hopefulness. "Couldn't we have a stove?"

"Have sense," said father, "how could we get a stove over that track?"

How indeed? For the road, though gradually creeping nearer, was still six miles away, and all our possessions had to come to us on pack horses over an unformed track. Gallant old nags, they would slip and slide on the steep hills, cleverly avoiding the projecting roots of the trees, twisting and turning through the bush to avoid trees and boulders.

"No," said father, cheerfully. "We'll have a nice colonial oven."

Mother sighed. She had had sixteen years of cooking with a colonial oven in a previous pioneering experience. As for me, there was just one thing on earth I desired, and that was a stove. My sister and I did not refrain from mentioning the matter to our friends, and so far succeeded in awakening public sympathy and interest that a number of neighbours undertook to carry in a stove for us. On a certain Sunday morning we girls, thrilled to the marrow, rode up the track to witness the progess of the stove and its bearers. Threading its way through the bush we saw slowly advancing towards us what at first sight looked like a funeral cortege. Firmly lashed to poles and enthroned on bracken was *the* stove, borne along by six stalwarts, including father. Our horses, giving one startled look at this apparition, wheeled and bolted and needed much coercion to bring them back. Relieved every now and then by others, the men continued on their way up hill and down, through mossy glades where tangled roots of trees made walking difficult, through deep mud, over a bridge none too secure. Home at last, and Mother's smiling face and the kettle singing, and the table spread! What a merry meal that was!

[Raetihi, Brave Days, Pioneer Women of New Zealand, 1939]

ISBN: 9780170230766

How to make a glossary

Think about identity, culture and organisation: how people pass on and sustain culture and heritage for different reasons and how this has results for people.

A **glossary** usually appears at the back of text such as a book and contains specialised or uncommon terms and words in alphabetical order with their meanings that appear in the text. These are terms that the writer knows well, but the reader may never have heard before. For example, if you did not play cricket you might not know a *yorker* is a ball, usually fast, pitched close to the batsman.

Practice 1

Study the chart about the economy of New Zealand at one particular month. It probably contains many terms you don't know. Highlight ten terms that should appear in a glossary to go with the text. Number each term to show the order in which terms should be listed in the glossary.

Skill: Recognising technical terms
- Don't worry if you can't understand terms. Even experts have trouble trying to explain what things like the Gini index mean.
- If the term is an abbreviation, use the first letter as the guide for where it should go in the list.
- Always note where data comes from. The *CIA World Factbook* makes a profile for every country and because it uses US dollars you can easily compare statistics of different countries.
- Think about how the British introduced money and imports and exports to New Zealand and how this economic system has been passed on down the generations.

Economy of New Zealand	
[Source: *CIA World Factbook, March 2012, US Dollars*]	
Currency	1 New Zealand Dollar (NZD) = 100 cents
Fiscal year	1 April – 31 March
Trade organisations	APEC, WTO, OECD
GDP (purchasing power parity)	$123.3 billion
GDP per capita	$27,900
GDP by sector	agriculture 4.7%, industry 24%, services 71.3%
Inflation (CPI)	4.5%
Gini index	36.2
Labour force	2.35 million
Unemployment	6.5%
Ease of doing business	Ranked 3rd
Exports	$40.92 billion
Imports	$35.07 billion
Public debt	33.7% of GDP
Electricity production	42 billion kWh
Oil production	60,480 bbl/day

ISBN: 9780170230766

Practice 2

Read this text about early Maori. Make a glossary that would save the writer having to explain in the text the meanings of Maori terms.

The Polynesian ancestors of early Maori voyaged from Hawaiki, their ancestral homeland, in waka which were traditional canoes. In New Zealand, which they called Aotearoa, they became tangata whenua or people of the land. Papatuanuku, land, was their ancestor and on it they established a place for their feet – their turangawaewae. Natural features were important and names descriptive; for example, rua meaning hole with pehu meaning to explode made Ruapehu, and roto meaning lake with rua meaning two made Rotorua. Gods had links with the land. Tane was god of trees and birds, Haumiatiketike was god of the fern root. Some places could be tapu or forbidden. The land gave Maori taonga, treasures, such as a pounamu mere which was a greenstone club, and food such as kiore the Pacific rat, kuri the Polynesian dog, birds such as moa, keruru the pigeon and titi the muttonbird. The land even cooked some of the food in a hangi, an underground oven. Tohunga whakairo, who were carvers, worked with wood from the land, and houses called whare, and the carved meeting house known as whare whakairo featured many materials from the land.

ISBN: 9780170230766

How to make a timeline

Think about continuity and change: how events have causes and results.

A **timeline** is a line or list of events with dates to show when and in what order events happened during a particular time period. For example, a timeline of Ancient Greece would show the key events of that time. Events are written briefly, such as 776 BC First Olympic Games, at Olympia in Greece.

Practice 1

Study the following text and highlight events and dates you would use to make a timeline about nuclear disasters. Put a number beside each event to show the order of events on the timeline.

Skill: Listing events for a timeline
- Because writers do not always mention events in the order in which they happened you need to do detective work to get the order.
- Look for dates and the events that happened at those dates. The timeline will give only the most essential information about the event, such as the numbers of people affected.
- Think about how each of these disasters had causes and results, and how some results are still being felt today.

Asia has well over a hundred nuclear power plants and many more planned, with the greatest growth expected in China, Japan, South Korea and India although countries such as Pakistan and Malaysia, Thailand and Vietnam, Bangladesh and Indonesia either have nuclear reactors built or partially built or planned. However, the Japanese history of nuclear disasters, particular the 2011 disaster at Fukushima that followed an earthquake and tsunami, has made many countries reconsider their nuclear futures. Two Japanese nuclear accidents were at Tokaimura – in 1997 when 37 people were exposed to radiation, and 1999 when two people died and about 100 were sent to hospital for exposure to radiation. Over 270 people were affected by radioactive leaks at Tsuruga in 1981 and four people died from radioactive leaks at Mihama in 2004. In terms of deaths, the 2011 disaster, with its equipment failures, nuclear meltdowns, release of radioactive materials, four immediate deaths and tens of thousands forced to leave the area, was not the worst in the world. When the Chernobyl plant blew up in the Ukraine in 1986 around 200 people were seriously contaminated and within three months 32 had died. Over 350,000 people were shifted out of the area. Experts still argue over the number of deaths expected in the future from this accident. In Kyshtym in Russia, around 10,000 people were evacuated in 1957 when reports surfaced of people's skin falling off after an accident, and radiation is estimated to have led to the death of 200 people there. The accident at Cumberland in 1957, Britain's first nuclear reactor, was blamed for an estimated 200 cancer cases, half of them fatal.

ISBN: 9780170230766

Practice 2

Read the text about Maori myths and legends and in the blank space underneath it make a timeline to show the key events.

Skill: Making a timeline

- Work out times for the beginning and end of the timeline. Distances between events will be approximate only as there are few dates known. Look for clue words such as before and later, after and then, to work out the order of events.
- Events often appear on a timeline in the present tense; for example, Polynesians <u>leave</u> Hawaiki rather than Polynesians <u>left</u> Hawaiki.
- The timeline can be a straight vertical or horizontal line, a line that goes both vertically and horizontally, a curved line like a road, or just a list, especially if the timeline covers a long time such as centuries.
- Make up a title for the timeline.
- Think about how some events are mysteries because we don't know everything about them.

To explain how the world began, Maori have creation stories, called myths and legends because they involve events that are said to have happened before scientific evidence can be found for them. Likewise, scientists are still searching for evidence to establish dates for traditions that tell of how Polynesians came to settle in Aotearoa/New Zealand. Firstly, there was only Te Kore, darkness and nothingness. Out of this came Ranginui, the Sky father, and Papatuanuku, the Earth mother. They had many children who were locked in darkness between their parents until they separated the parents. Later, a demi-god called Maui became the fifth son to be born to his parents in Hawaiki. He had magic powers that not everyone in his family knew about. One day he hid in a canoe so he could go fishing with his brothers and by the time the brothers discovered him they were far from land. With his magic fishhook Maui fished up Te Ika a Maui, the North Island of New Zealand. Te Waka a Maui is the South Island and Te Punga a Maui is Stewart Island. However, it was the great Polynesian navigator Kupe, who lived in Hawaiki, who is said to have discovered Aotearoa in about 925 AD. He then returned to Hawaiki with instructions on how to get to this new land and this allowed Toi and Whatonga to arrive in about 1150 AD. Tradition says that about 200 years later came the great fleet, about eight canoes from Hawaiki.

ISBN: 9780170230766

How to make a star diagram

Think about the economic world: how producers and consumers exercise their rights and meet their responsibilities and how economic decisions impact on people, communities and nations.

A useful tool to help you take notes, brainstorm or study is a **star diagram**. The middle box, or circle or star point, contains the topic and the surrounding boxes contain points about the topic. There can be as many or as few boxes as you want.

Shellfish and fish are contaminated.

Oil washes up on beaches.

Possible results of an oil spill at sea.

Birds get coated in oil.

Local businesses have to close.

Practice 1

Read the text about Fair trade. Highlight words you would use in a star diagram to summarise the text.

Skill: Finding evidence

- Think of your topic box containing a statement; for example, *Fair trade is a social movement*. Then look for evidence that proves that statement.
- As it is a summary, keep evidence brief; for example, *Aims for better deal for producers*.
- Imagine how it might feel to at last get a decent wage for your work in a tea plantation if you were in a poor country, and how it might feel to at last earn your Fairtrade Certification Mark as an owner of an export company in a developed country.

Fair trade is an organised social movement whose aim is to get a better deal for producers of goods in developing countries such as the many poor ones in Africa. Examples of Fair trade goods are handicrafts, coffee, cocoa, sugar, tea, bananas, honey, cotton, wine, chocolate, flowers, gold, oranges, cocoa, shortbread, dried and fresh fruits and vegetables, juices, nuts, oil seeds, rice, spices, footballs, rum, beer, cereal bars and muesli. To win the Fairtrade Certification Mark, companies in developed countries such as New Zealand wanting to buy goods from developing countries must pay producers higher-than-the-market- price for products and ensure goods are produced in an environmentally-friendly way. Fair trade also promotes a safe and healthy working environment for producers including children like the child gold miners who live and work in mines with high levels of pollution. Producers of many Fair trade goods work in homes or villages, often in remote areas with few resources which means that they have no factories or cargo planes causing pollution and they get a chance to earn money. Fair trade is one of the most debated topics in economics with some experts saying it helps developing countries and some saying it has little effect.

ISBN: 9780170230766

Practice 2

Use the star diagram to summarise the information about the Fairtrade Certification Mark.

Skill: Describing
- Make sure you understand key terms, **certification** = something like a document, certificate, mark, logo that shows standards have been met.
- Try to find answers to *When*, *Where*, *Who*, *What*, *Why*, *How* to make sure you have got the main points.
- Think about how the Fairtrade Certification Mark is a symbol for both producers and consumers.

Companies that offer goods that meet Fairtrade standards can apply to use the Fairtrade Certification Mark as a visible promise that producers in the developing world are getting a fairer deal. Created in 2002 and now used in many countries, it is growing in popularity as Fairtrade sales continue to rise around the world. The Mark represents a person cheering or waving against a background of green grass and blue sky, celebrating a fair deal and knowing he or she is making a positive difference by being involved in fair trade. The black dot and swirl at the centre is the person holding one arm aloft and this person represents both producers and consumers at the heart of the Fairtrade system – perhaps a farmer holding up produce, or a shopper reaching for a product, or a campaigner fighting for more fairness in international trade. Underneath is the term FAIRTRADE written in white letters against the black background.

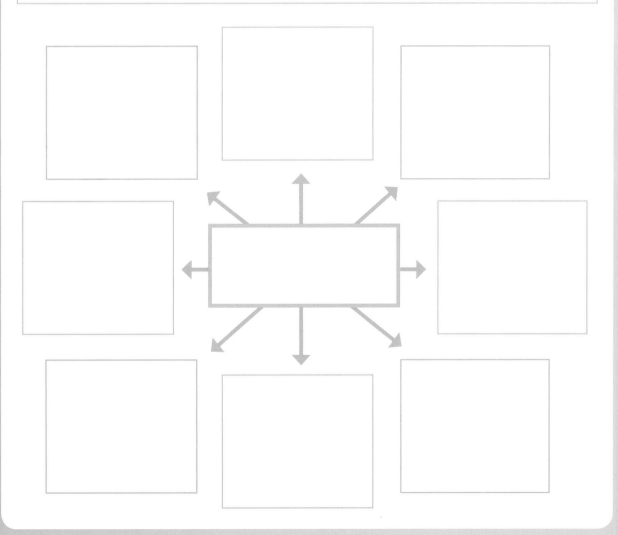

ISBN: 9780170230766

How to answer multi-choice questions

Think about the economic world: how people's management of resources impacts on environmental and social sustainability.

The way to do well in a multi-choice test is to know your material well so you are confident of answers. However, sometimes you may be asked to answer questions on text you have not read before. This calls for **reasoning** which is forming conclusions by using evidence.

Practice 1

Skill: Reasoning
- Read the text carefully. Decide if biofuel will have positive or negative effects.
- Read questions carefully. An answer that seems silly is probably incorrect. Look for possible traps; for example, *what is the difference between biofuel and biokerosene*? (There is no difference.)
- Use detective work, for example, *What is Charles de Gaulle linked with*?
- If you don't lose points for incorrect answers, answer all the questions even if this means having an educated guess.

Study the text below and answer the questions that follow.

Biofuel is produced from renewable biological material such as plants. In 2011 KLM Royal Dutch Airlines (Koninklijke Luchtwaart Maatschappij) announced plans to recycle used cooking oil into biofuel for flights to and from Paris in order to improve sustainability and lower carbon dioxide emissions. In June the carrier ran a scheduled flight between Amsterdam Schiphol and Paris Charles de Gaulle on a blend of biokerosene derived from cooking oil and jet fuel. The oil came from factories and hotels and no changes had to be made to engines or aircraft infrastructure.

1   The closest word to recycle is

　　a) reduce　　　　　　　　b) reuse　　　　　　　　c) refuse.

2   Koninklijke Luchtwaart Maatschappij is most likely to be the

　　a) airline　　　　　　　　b) biofuel　　　　　　　c) carbon.

3   The word that means using wisely so there is enough for future generations is

　　a) infrastructure　　　　　b) emissions　　　　　　c) sustainability.

4   The carrier believes that lowering carbon dioxide emissions is

　　a) a disadvantage　　　　b) an advantage　　　　c) not an aim.

5   The June flight was

　　a) a normal planned one　　b) an exhibition one　　c) a one-off demonstration one.

6   The use of biofuel described here is best described as

　　a) traditional　　　　　　b) modern　　　　　　　c) unsustainable.

7   Charles de Gaulle is most likely to have been a leader of

　　a) Netherlands　　　　　b) Schiphol　　　　　　c) France.

8   The most likely outfit the KLM airline merged with in 2003 is

　　a) Air New Zealand　　　b) Air Italy　　　　　　c) Air France.

9 The biofuel will most help the airline's

    a) carbon footprint   b) infrastructure   c) overweight passengers.

10 Globally, most benefit of the biofuel will go to the

    a) passengers   b) environment   c) cooking oil manufacturers.

Practice 2

Read the text below and answer the questions that follow.

Skill: Reasoning
- Make sure you understand key words; for example, **debris** = scattered rubbish, **marine** = to do with the sea.
- Read the text carefully and decide if the plastic has positive OR negative effects.
- Read questions carefully and look for clue words; for example, probably means likely but not definitely.
- Notice words that give location; for example, globally means around the world.

Much of the world's plastic ends up in the sea as marine debris. About 80 percent comes from land and the rest from vessels. In certain places, such as the Central Pacific Gyre, currents concentrate the debris. Plastic kills many fish and birds, harms coral reefs and experts think toxins that get into the food-chain affect human hormones and are linked to trends such as higher ratios of females to males. They say the problem is so bad it is probably unfixable. Instead of biodegrading and decomposing away, plastic breaks down into pieces that are still plastic, even though pieces can be invisible.

1 Generally, plastic marine debris is

    a) helpful   b) harmful   c) both helpful and harmful.

2 The majority of marine plastic debris comes from

    a) boats   b) ships   c) land.

3 The closest word in meaning to toxic is

    a) poisonous   b) plastic   c) chemical.

4 The most likely word to mean breaking down by bacteria rather than light is

    a) photodegrades   b) biodegrades   c) marinedegrades.

5 A gyre is most likely to be a

    a) graveyard under the sea   b) circular motion   c) seagulls' feeding zone.

6 The writer seems to suggest marine plastic debris may be

    a) the new toxic time-bomb   b) best left to experts   c) mainly a Pacific problem.

7 The concentration of plastic in vast garbage patches is caused by

    a) coral reefs   b) currents   c) grandparents.

8 Floating plastics concentrate chemicals which

    a) get in the food chain   b) affect sea creatures   c) both of these.

9 The most-environmentally-friendly place for plastic rubbish at the beach is

    a) buried in sand   b) on rocks uncovered   c) with people to go home.
                                      at low tide

10 Experts suggest clearing the ocean of plastic may be

    a) too difficult   b) necessary   c) pointless.

ISBN: 9780170230766

Problem-solving

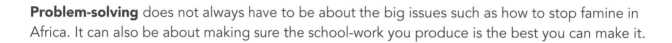

Think about place and environment: how people move between places and how this has reults for the people and places.

Problem-solving does not always have to be about the big issues such as how to stop famine in Africa. It can also be about making sure the school-work you produce is the best you can make it.

Practice 1

Study the text below and do the activities that follow.

Skill: Being consistent

- Although you are a few years away from university, it helps to know that when in doubt use British rather than American spelling. Some markers insist only that you are consistent; for example, you have all British spelling or all American spelling. You probably won't lose marks for using a mix of British and American spellings but if you learn about being consistent now in this one area, it will help you to be consistent elsewhere. Consistency makes your work look tidy and well-organised.
- Think about how the movement of people can have effects on things you would perhaps never imagine, such as spelling.

Immigration words and spelling

Migrate = go from one country, region or place to settle in another country, region or place. People and animals can migrate. **Emigrate** = to leave your country to settle in another. People, but not animals, emigrate. **Immigrate** = to come into a new country of which you are not a native in order to live there. People, but not animals, immigrate. **Emigration** = the act of emigrating. **Immigration** = the act of immigrating.

After British settlers immigrated to America they developed spellings of some words that were different to how the British spelled them. Americans, for example, tended to spell words more closely to how they sounded and to leave out some letters. This can be confusing for New Zealanders because we follow the British spelling but read a lot of material from the US, especially on the net.

Some spelling differences between British and American English

British	American	British	American	British	American
harbour	harbor	gaol	jail	enquire	inquire
centre	center	discs	disks	labelled	labeled
kilometre	kilometer	analyse	analyze	storey	story
archaeology	archeology	sceptic	skeptic	grey	gray
civilisation	civilization	judgement	judgment	travelled	traveled

ISBN: 9780170230766

1 Circle the word in the following pairs that is most likely to be British spelling.

plow/plough   acclimatise/acclimatize   program/programme   meter/metre

aluminum/aluminium   colonize/colonise   mediaeval/medieval   offence/offense

2 In the spaces provided put either Migration, Immigration or Emigration that best describes the action involved.

a Sean fled from Ireland. _____

b Godwits fly between New Zealand and Alaska. _____

c British came to live in New Zealand in the 19th century. _____

d Jews escaped Nazi Germany. _____

e Movement to do with the point of the destination. _____

f Movement to do with the point of departure. _____

g Polynesians from Hawaiki settled in New Zealand. _____

Practice 2

Study the Push/Pull Factors Chart below which is a problem-solving exercise to do with emigration and immigration. Then colour the PUSH factors one colour and PULL factors another colour.

Skill: Classifying

- Factors pushing people to leave a country are push factors while factors pulling people to enter a country are pull factors. If you ran up gambling debts in 19th century England your family might offer to pay you a monthly allowance if you emigrated which was a push factor. When you immigrated to New Zealand rather than Canada because the winter weather is better, that was a pull factor in operation.
- Make sure you understand key words; for example, **persecution** = to illtreat someone especially because of religion, beliefs, race, gender.
- Think about how these push and pull factors will affect the people and places concerned.

Political persecution.	Search for adventure.	Religious persecution.
A chance to own land.	Escape a natural disaster.	Get a better education.
Boredom.	Find a better job.	Find a job.
Escape a man-made disaster.	Run away from family.	Better cultural environment.
Start life again where nobody knows you.	Offer from another country to pay travel expenses.	Family pays for you to live in a different country.
Dislike of government.	Get better medical care.	Sporting opportunity.
Better climate.	Escape civil war.	Exiled by government.
Other family members have already migrated to a particular country.		Doctor insists you have a change of environment.
Rising sea level.	Desire to flee a personal tragedy.	No freedom of speech.
Escape the law.	Hunger, starvation, famine.	Better tax deal.

ISBN: 9780170230766

22 Knowing events have causes and effects

Think about continuity and change: how events have causes and effects.

An event is something that takes place or happens. Famous events in New Zealand include the signing of the Treaty of Waitangi in 1840, women getting the right to vote in 1893, Edmund Hillary climbing Mt Everest in 1953 and the Christchurch earthquake of 2011. A skill to learn is how to work out the **causes** and **effects** of an event.

CAUSE	EFFECT
• makes the event happen • comes before the event.	• happens as a result of the event • comes after the event.

A cause of the Christchurch earthquake was that New Zealand is at the boundary between two tectonic plates and plate movements drive earthquakes. An effect of the earthquake was that 185 people died.

Practice 1

On the chart below are eight causes, eight events and eight effects; each cause and each effect is linked with one event. The events are in red. Write 'cause' or 'effect' in each non-red box and use colours or arrows to show which cause and effect belong together and to which event they both belong.

Skill: Linking
- Look for words and ideas that show three things in the boxes are related.
- To work out causes, ask 'Why did the event happen?' To work out effects, ask 'What were the results of the event?'
- Think about how cause and effect are linked and how the cause is often a decision and the effect is often an impact on people's lives.

World War 2 started.	Two tectonic plates moved against each other.	The Industrial Revolution began.	European explorers reached New Zealand.
A Quota Management system was set up.	An annual Pasifika Festival is held in Auckland.	Bad economic times made Germans look for a saviour.	Commercial passenger air travel began.
An underwater earthquake occurred.	There are rich countries and poor countries.	Tourism became a big earner in NZ's economy.	Scientists warned about over-fishing.

ISBN: 9780170230766

People invented big machines that fitted only in big buildings.	Many Pacific Islanders migrated to New Zealand.	The Treaty of Waitangi was signed.	Resources were not evenly distributed.
Nature ignores political borders.	Some fish stocks in New Zealand waters started to run out.	A tsunami killed thousands.	Hitler came to power in Germany.
The Wright brothers and others made flight possible.	People moved to towns to work in factories.	Europeans began to settle in New Zealand.	Pacific Islanders looked for a better economic future.

Practice 2

Read the text below about the Wairau Affair and highlight causes in one colour and effects in another colour.

Skill: Locating and grouping
- Check you understand key words; for example, **affair** = event, **massacre** = brutal killing or slaughter.
- A writer might mention some effects of an event before mentioning some causes.
- Locate and group by working out what came before the violence (the causes) and what came after (the effects).
- Think about what life would have been like in 1843 without modern technology and when two cultural groups were impacting on each other, sometimes with violence caused by misunderstandings.

The Wairau Affair took place in New Zealand on 17 June 1843; four Maori died and three were wounded; twenty-two Europeans died and five were wounded. The New Zealand Company, which was settling British settlers on land, believed it had bought land from Maori in the Wairau Valley. The Maori, led by chiefs Te Rauparaha and Te Rangihaeta, challenged the land sale. Because they wanted the Land Commissioner to check out the facts of the matter, they tried to stop the survey of the land and destroyed the surveyors' equipment and shelters that the surveyors had made from resources on the land, such as wooden pegs and thatched huts. A group of about 50 British set off from Nelson to arrest the two chiefs. They found about 90 Maori at the Tuamarina Stream. The chiefs refused to leave. Firing broke out and Te Rongo, a wife of Te Rangihaeta and daughter of Te Rauparaha, was killed. Te Rangihaeta demanded utu and the British who had surrendered were killed. This horrified people in Britain and British settlers in New Zealand and they called the event the Wairau Massacre. Newspapers published inaccurate reports and settlers became unwilling to buy land. The British Governor tried to calm down anger between Maori and British and carried out an investigation of the affair. Maori, including the two chiefs, were invited to give their version of the affair. The Governor decided the British had been in the wrong and so he would not avenge their deaths, although he told the chiefs they had committed a crime when they killed men who had surrendered. The finding made the Governor unpopular with the British settlers and he was replaced.

ISBN: 9780170230766

Think about continuity and change: how people take part as individuals and in groups to respond to community challenges.

During and after an event people have things to say about it. Examples are giving interviews for newspapers, writing in diaries, taking photographs, painting pictures, making movies, sending emails or making speeches, writing novels or non-fiction books, drawing maps, texting. The interviews, diary entries and so on are called resources or sources. Resources created at the time of an event by a person who was present or alive at the time are known as **primary resources**.

Practice 1

Read the resource below about the Wairau Affair and underline all the words that show this is a primary resource.

Skill: Investigating
- To investigate if it is a primary resource ask yourself, *How does the person know details about the event?* *Is the person an eyewitness* (saw it with his/her own eyes)? *Does the person use words like I, we, us, our?*
- Imagine what it would have been like at the hearing before the Lands Claims Commissioner in 1843 when the clash was still fresh in people's minds.

"Rangihaeata persisted in going to Wairau, which we did. We told the surveyors not to work any more and go away; that we would not allow them to do anything more till we were paid for our land but they took no notice of us. We went again to their stations and told them to take their things out of the house. They would not - but we did, and put them in their boat, burnt the house and took the white people to the entrance of the river and left them at the Pa. We went up to the river to a creek Tua Marina and were there clearing the land for potatoes when I saw the Victoria laying off the mouth of the Wairau. Next morning when we had done eating some of my men said there were Pakeha coming towards us. We assembled men, women, and children on the bank of the river to see and hear what the Pakehas wanted. They all got on the brow of a fern hill and stood.

Then part of them came to the bank of the river and called for a canoe which was given them. Mr Thompson, Capt.Wakefield, Capt. England, Mr Cotterill, Mr Tuckett, Brook the interpreter, the constable and others came over to us.

I told him [Thompson] I burnt nothing of theirs; it was my own; the grass and wood that grew on my land! And I would not go with him. It would be good to talk of the matter there - what odds if it did occupy two or three days - I would let them have the land when they paid me for it. He [Thompson] would not listen to me he turned away to the constable and got handcuffs, and then came to me taking me by the hand. When I found what he wanted I snatched my hand away from his. He got very angry and said if I did not come he would fire on us. I said don't be foolish we don't want to fight ...Puaha (Rawiri) rose with a testament in his hand saying to the Pakehas: "Don't fire on us; we are Christians and do not want to fight". When the Pakehas got to the top of the hill they waved a white handkerchief to make peace. I could not get up the hill fast - the young

ISBN: 9780170230766

men ran before me, shooting and cutting down Pakehas as they ran away. I called to them to spare the gentlemen, but Rangihaeata coming up behind me at the time said "why save them - they have shot your daughter." When I heard that my voice failed me. Rangihaeata got up the hill and all the Pakehas were killed."

[Account by Te Rauparaha made to the Land Claims Commissioner on 1 July 1843.]

Practice 2

Now read the account again and answer the questions that follow.

Skill: Verifying
- **Verifying** means you look for new evidence to back up your opinion. You will have decided that the text is a primary resource and now you are to search for further proof.
- Make sure you understand actions; for example, waving a white handkerchief was often used in place of a white flag to show surrender or desire to end fighting.
- Imagine what it would have been like being at the clash as either a Maori warrior or a British soldier.

1 What punctuation marks show this is somebody talking?
_____

2 Which two groups of people were involved in the event?
_____
_____

3 Who is the speaker? _____

4 What reason is given for the speaker being at the scene of the event?
_____
_____

5 To which group does he belong? _____

6 Give a reason he is the speaker. _____
_____

7 To whom is he speaking? _____
_____

8 When was the account made? _____

9 How does that date compare to the date of the event?
_____

10 Is this an eyewitness account? Give a reason for your answer.
_____
_____

11 List the people mentioned by name in the account and put a tick or cross beside them to show if the speaker ever met or saw them.
_____
_____
_____
_____

12 List the places and vessel mentioned by name and put a tick or cross beside them to show if the speaker ever saw them.
_____
_____

ISBN: 9780170230766

Knowing secondary resources

Think about continuity and change: how people remember and record the past in different ways.

Generally, **secondary resources** are created after an event and by a person who was either not alive at the time of the event or not involved in it.

Practice 1

Tick what are most likely to be secondary resources on the chart below.

Skill: Investigating and grouping
- To investigate if it is a secondary resource ask, How does the person know details about the event? Has the person found out about the event much later?
- Imagine how all the different ways of remembering and recording the past can make it confusing sometimes to work out exactly what happened.

news film footage		PowerPoint presentation		Wikipedia		religious sermon	
reference book		text message		black box from a plane		The Diary of Anne Frank	
trial transcript		postcard		minutes of a meeting		letter	
autobiography		the Treaty of Waitangi		TV series about Ancient Greece		fieldwork	
book about the history of money		biography		encyclopaedia		will	
divorce record		memoir		public opinion poll		birth certificate	
article about the history of whaling		'My Struggle' written by Hitler		book about Hitler written in 2000		film about the 1347 Black Death	
interview with tsunami survivor		marriage certificate		history textbook		legal contract	
article about Maori homeland Hawaiki		CD-ROM		NZ census statistics		book on explorers throughout history	
message in a bottle		time capsule		newspaper		television news broadcast	
soldier's paybook		receipt		invoice - bill		bus timetable	
souvenir booklet		story about dinasours		protest placard		speech in Parliament	
United Nations Declaration of Human Rights		voter registry		coin		newspaper advertisement	
email		ship's log .		constitution of the USA		movie poster	

ISBN: 9780170230766

Practice 2

Read the text below about the Wairau Affair and do the activities that follow.

Skill: Interpreting different points of view
- Secondary resources tend to give an overview rather than an inside view.
- Writers sometimes use emotive language which is charged with feeling and designed to cause an emotional reaction from readers.

At first the Maoris contented themselves with pulling up the surveyors' pegs; but, when the surveyors had been at work for four or five weeks, Rauparaha appeared with a hundred men and drove them away. When the fugitive surveyors arrived at Nelson, Captain Wakefield acted swiftly. A warrant was issued for the arrest of the two principal chiefs on a charge of arson and the chief magistrate, with an escort of thirty, set out for the scene of the outrage. They were going to settle with these bullies once and for all.

As it was not expected that the chiefs would offer resistance no members of the escort were sworn in as special constables and the labourers were simply told that they were going "assist the surveyors"; but once in the Wairau Valley arms were issued for the sake of appearance, and the party proceeded up the river, uneasily handling "firelocks and bayonets or fowling-pieces and cutlasses". Few of them had ever handled a gun before and some of them had no ammunition. They found the Maoris, the two wanted men and a party of eighty supporters, on the far side of a deep and swift little stream and the leaders went over in a boat (shoved across by the Maoris) to make the arrest. They went without arms, but the constable carried a pair of handcuffs. When Rauparaha refused to go with them, the chief magistrate grew very excited and, pointing to his armed escort across the stream, said that in that case they would have to use force. In the midst of great noise and excitement, the leaders pushed the boat back athwart the stream to enable the armed men to come over and five of them stepped in; and then somehow – nobody knows precisely what happened – a musket went off and fighting started. The Europeans were quite unready for a real fight and most of them scattered; but the wife of one of the chiefs had been killed and the Maori blood was up, and in the wild hunt that followed twenty-three Europeans were killed.

[New Zealand by Harold Miller, 1950, Hutchinson's University Library, London]

1   List three reasons for calling this a secondary resource.

   a _____
   _____
   b _____
   _____
   c _____
   _____

2   Highlight three emotive words or groups of words.

3   Underline three people who appear in both the primary and secondary resources about this event.

ISBN: 9780170230766

25 How to sort out fact and opinion

Think about the economic world: how people look for and have looked for economic growth through business, enterprise (project that might be difficult, bold, needing energy) and innovation (newness).

Being able to sort out what are facts and what are opinions speeds up your research and means you have a better chance of finding accurate information.

fact = something that really happened or is true and accurate eg. The Treaty of Waitangi was signed in 1840.
opinion = something that is a personal belief or judgement eg. The Treaty of Waitangi makes New Zealand a great country.

Practice 1

Read the text about the OECD. Highlight the facts in one colour and the opinions in another colour.

Skill: Distinguishing
- Distinguish between fact and opinion by asking: *Would everyone agree with this statement or is it just the speaker or writer's own judgement?*
- Think about why not every country would want to belong to the OECD.

The OECD publishes many statistics. Not enough people know what OECD means. It stands for Organisation for Economic Cooperation and Development. In 2011 it had 34 countries as members, including New Zealand and Australia. Membership is not automatically available to any country who wants it. The OECD aims to encourage economic progress and world trade. All its members believe in democracy. It tries to find answers to economic problems. It may have been a reasonable idea at the time it was set up but it has not achieved much. One thing New Zealand gets out of being a member is that every two years the OECD releases an economic review of New Zealand. This review is just telling Kiwis what they already know. The ideas for turning our economy around don't seem practical. But it could be useful to have outside eyes looking over our economy and offering suggestions.

Practice 2

Study the diagram and the commentary on the diagram. Then do the activities on the next page.

Skill: Checking
- Make sure you know the meaning of terms; for example, **median** = middle value in a list, **life expectancy** = average period someone can expect to live, **obesity** = excess body fat, **tertiary education** = after secondary school, **GDP** = Gross Domestic Product (total value of all goods and services produced in a country in a given year), **perceived** = regarded, **discrimination** = unfair treatment based on something like religion or race, **corruption** = dishonest behaviour by someone in power.
- Sometimes people get their 'facts' wrong. A fact can be tested to see if it is true or not, whereas an opinion can't be tested.
- Think about how New Zealand compares with other countries.

ISBN: 9780170230766

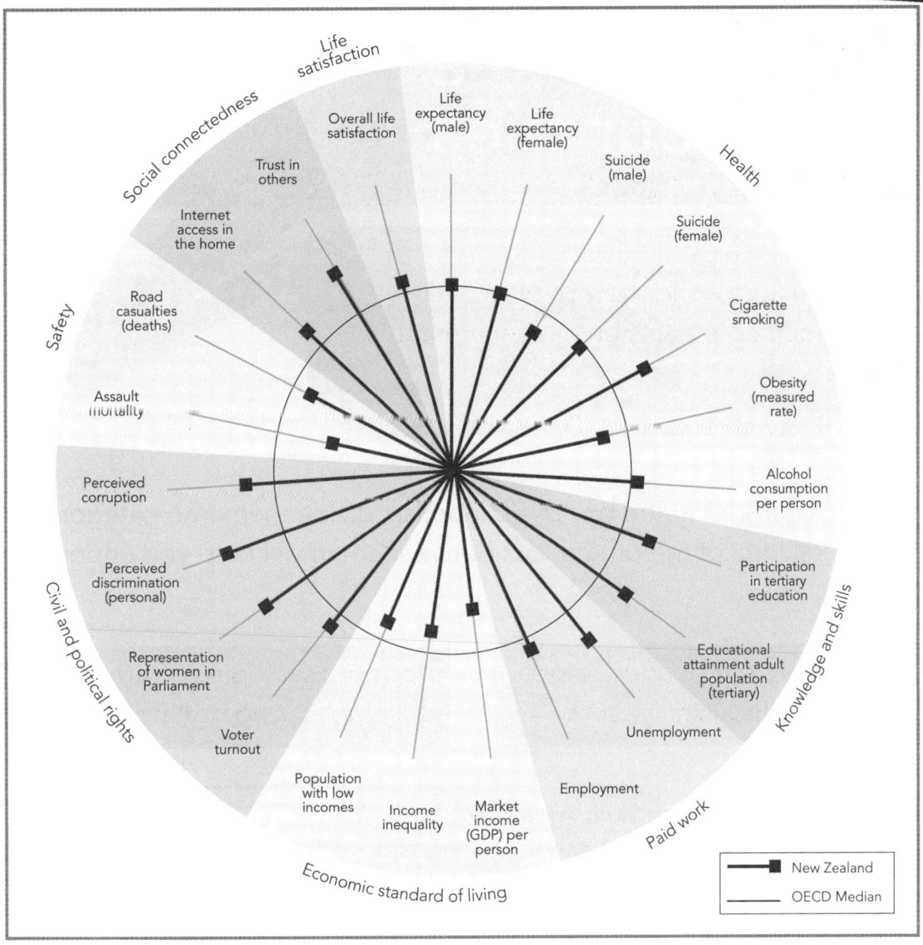

Diagram legend:
- New Zealand
- OECD Median

1. The writer of the commentary did not take long enough to check facts and has made several mistakes. Check the original primary document to see which 'facts' the person has got wrong. Put a tick or cross in each box on the commentary to show this.

2. The commentary also contains two opinions. Highlight these.

3. The person who wrote the commentary would have been free to post it on the net. What does this suggest about information available on the net?

_____

_____

Commentary on the diagram

☐ New Zealanders' overall life satisfaction is lower than the median.

☐ New Zealand performed very well in the Safety area.

☐ New Zealanders' internet access is higher than the median; this shows Kiwis spend too much time on computers.

☐ New Zealand's economic standard of living results tend to be higher than the median.

☐ In the health area New Zealand's results are mixed.

☐ New Zealand has relatively high suicide death rates but rates of cigarette smoking and alcohol consumption are lower than the median.

☐ New Zealand's life expectancy is similar to the median.

☐ New Zealand has a long way to go to reach the median in knowledge and skills.

☐ New Zealanders' trust in others is above the median.

☐ New Zealand's unemployment is above the median.

☐ New Zealand performs well in civil and potitical rights; Kiwis should feel proud.

ISBN: 9780170230766

26 Understanding rich and poor countries

Think about the economic world: how people's management of resources impacts on environmental and social sustainability.

There are about 196 countries in the world. Economists divide them into categories such as rich and poor. Having a general idea of the differences between them will help you understand topics to do with economics.

Rich = developed, first-world, most developed, and industrialised.

Poor = developing, Third World, least developed, and not industrialised.

Practice 1

Study the characteristics in the chart below. Choose which ones are more likely to belong to poor countries and colour these one colour. Colour the ones more likely to belong to rich countries another colour.

Skill: Assigning
- Each time you assign a characteristic to a country, be aware it is a general comment only and there will be exceptions; for example, Switzerland is a rich country yet it has few natural resources - its economy is largely based around science and technology.
- Make sure you understand key terms; for example, **mortality** = death, **subsistence** = growing food for just your family, **illiteracy** = unable to read or write, **cycle of poverty** = poor families trapped in poverty for generations and will stay poor until outside help breaks the cycle.
- Think about how the way countries manage resources impacts on their environment and society; for example, if New Zealand had no central government or local government working, its environment and society would suffer.

Unsafe drinking water.	Job opportunities.	High infant mortality rate.	Attracts overseas investors.	Low school enrolment rates.
Adequate food.	Poor health care.	Illiteracy.	High HIV rates.	Poor technology.
High life expectancy at birth.	Government maintains law and order.	Few resources to cope with natural disasters.	Dependent on small number of exports.	Little or no overseas investors.
Malnutrition and starvation.	No or little industry.	Subsistence farming.	High average income.	Responsible government.
Adequate health care.	Corrupt government.	Compulsory education.	No overpopulation.	Low infant mortality rate.
Industrialisation.	Peaceful society.	Low HIV rates.	Civil war.	Overpopulation.
Low average income.	Safe drinking water.	Few job opportunities.	Advanced technology.	Break-down of law and order.

ISBN: 9780170230766

Advanced science.	Few natural resources.	People feel hopeless.	Discrimination against females.	People have hope for the future.
High literacy rate.	Good transport and communications.	People are trapped in a cycle of poverty.	Reasonable supply of natural resources.	Little science.
Donates money to help other countries.	Unreliable transport and communications.	Welfare of people often depends on Aid groups.	Little or no effective central government.	Discrimination on grounds of sex is illegal.
Receives monetary help from other countries.	Government tries to prepare people to cope with natural disasters.	Large number of different exports.	Central government passes welfare laws to look after its citizens.	Work force is interested in working and earning money.

Practice 2

Choose the 25 countries from the following list that you believe are most likely to belong to the group of **developing** countries and colour them all the same colour. Colour the 25 countries that are most likely to belong to the group of **developed** countries a second colour.

Skill: Assessing

- Assess, or calculate, the chances of a country being rich or poor by thinking about its location. Africa and Asia have many poor countries. Europe has many rich countries. In the Pacific, New Zealand and Australia are rich countries.
- Being able to locate countries in the world is a good skill to have. You can learn the location of all the countries in the world by playing interactive games on the net such as *Sporcle*.
- Think about the many reasons why some countries are rich and others are poor; for example, a history of being taken over by a big power which used the resources of the country but did little to help it become independent and to develop its own economy.

AFGHANISTAN	AUSTRALIA	AUSTRIA	BANGLADESH	BELGIUM
BRAZIL	BURUNDI	CAMBODIA	CANADA	DENMARK
ERITREA	ETHIOPIA	FIJI	FINLAND	FRANCE
GAMBIA	GERMANY	GREECE	GUINEA	HAITI
ICELAND	IRELAND	ITALY	JAPAN	LIECHTENSTEIN
LUXEMBOURG	MALAWI	MONACO	MOZAMBIQUE	NEPAL
NETHERLANDS	NEW ZEALAND	NIGER	NORWAY	PAKISTAN
QATAR	RWANDA	SAMOA	SIERRA LEONE	SINGAPORE
SOLOMON ISLANDS	SOMALIA	SPAIN	SUDAN	SWEDEN
SWITZERLAND	TANZANIA	TOGO	TONGA	UGANDA
UNITED KINGDOM	UNITED STATES	VIETNAM	ZAMBIA	ZIMBABWE

ISBN: 9780170230766

How to find evidence

Think about the economic world: how people's management of resources, such as coal and money, impacts on environmental and social sustainability.

You will often be asked to find evidence from a resource such as a document to back up a statement. **Evidence** is something that shows whether a statement is true or not.

Statement	Evidence
New Zealand aims to be a bicultural country.	English and Maori are official languages.
British war-time leader Winston Churchill smoked cigars.	Photograph.
Gallipoli is located in Turkey.	Map.
The UN adopted the Universal Declaration of Human Rights in 1948.	Official document.

Practice 1

Use the resources about China's use and production of coal to give one piece of evidence for the statements that follow them.

Skill: Discovering and presenting

- Concentrate on the resources. You might know more about the topic than what is in the resources but you can't use your own knowledge – just what is in the resources.
- Discovering evidence in graphs can be more challenging than discovering it in text because you won't find it written in a sentence – you have to discover it and then present it in writing.
- Present evidence by referring to where you discovered it; for example, Resource 3 shows no other country produces as much coal as China …
- Think about how coal mining can be dangerous to workers and the environment and how using coal as fuel adds toxins to the atmosphere. Coal is also a non-renewable energy which means one day it could all be gone.

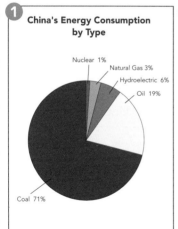

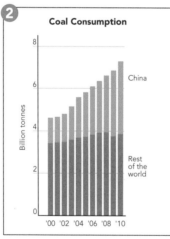

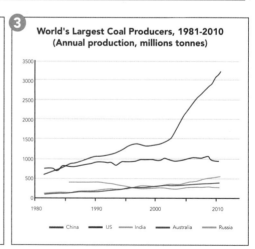

1 China dominates (rules) world coal production. _____

2 China's coal production has increased dramatically since 2000. _____

3 In 2010 China consumed 48 percent of the world's coal. _____

4 China's major energy use is coal. _____

_____

5 In 2010 the combined coal production of the US, India, Australia and Russia was less than that of China. _____

_____

Practice 2

Study the resources about inflation and find one piece of evidence for each of the statements.

Skill: Finding evidence
- The key to understanding inflation is in the first three sentences of Resource 2.
- Remember goods are products such as a smart phone; services are what people do for you such as mow the lawns.
- When presenting evidence you can quote directly from a resource; for example, *Resource 2 states that most economists …*
- Think about how the economy and inflation affects your life.

Resource 1

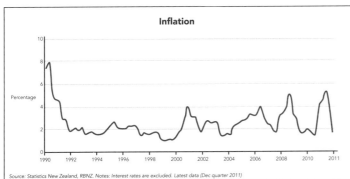

Source: Statistics New Zealand, RBNZ. Notes: Interest rates are excluded. Latest data (Dec quarter 2011)

Statements

1 Records are kept of inflation rates over the years.

_____

2 Inflation could be defined as demand in the economy outpacing supply. _____

_____

3 From 2000 to 2010 inflation rose and fell more than once. _____

_____

4 Not all economists agree on the best levels for inflation. _____

_____

5 Inflation is not just about goods. _____

_____

6 People on fixed incomes will suffer a decline in their standard of living during a period of inflation.

_____

_____

Resource 2: Economists use the term inflation to describe a rise of average prices. Inflation means money is losing its value, that what cost five dollars to buy two years ago may today cost eight dollars. It is usually caused by too much money being available to buy too few goods and services which means people can charge higher prices for goods and services. For example, at one period in 2011 prices of tomatoes rose 110 percent because supply from Australia fell during the Queensland floods. A rise in the cost of a basic good such as oil, brought in from overseas, can also cause inflation. If prices rise faster than incomes, inflation will hit people hard because money they earn buys less than it did. Most economists think inflation is best kept at a low, steady rate. This means that when an economic downturn hits, people and the economy have a better chance of coping.

ISBN: 9780170230766

How to write a paragraph

Think about the economic world: how people's management of resources impacts on environmental and social sustainability.

One of the most basic skills is being able to write a paragraph which is several sentences grouped together about a particular topic. You might have brilliant ideas and knowledge but if you can't write a paragraph you will struggle to communicate your ideas and knowledge.

Think of a paragraph as having three parts.

Part 1: The topic sentence. It is usually the first sentence and gives the general idea of what the paragraph is about, for example:

> One method that scientists use to work out the possible age of a very old object found in the soil, such as a Maori stone adze, is radiocarbon dating.

Part 2: The body sentences. They come after the topic sentence and support it by giving details and examples of it, for example:

> Scientists can test anything that was once alive such as wood and bone because it had carbon in it. If the object itself did not have carbon in it, scientists can test deposits at the place where the object was unearthed. For example, a Maori stone adze was recently unearthed in Porirua near the place believed to be where Kupe landed. Scientists used radiocarbon dating to test deposits at the place and said the place was probably used in the 15th century.

Part 3: The concluding sentence. The last sentence summarises the main idea, for example:

> By finding out how much of a particular carbon is in any object or deposit from the place in which it was found, scientists can work out how long ago the object was in existence.

Practice 1

Read the notes about the Great Depression of the 1930s in New Zealand and highlight with three different colours what you would use to help write the three parts of a paragraph on this topic.

Skill: Organising
- Make sure you understand key words; examples: **depression** = severe downturn of economic activity that lasts a long time, **bankruptcy** = person has no money to pay what is owed so is financially ruined.
- To organise the topic sentence, body sentences and concluding sentence think *Head, Body, Tail*.
- Imagine constantly being hungry or listening to your father describe how he had spent all day digging trenches and then filling them in because some of the relief schemes had no practical outcomes.

Notes about the Great Depression: Affected economies of most countries during 1930s. New Zealand depended on others, especially Britain, buying its goods such as meat and wool. Trade slowed, New Zealand farmers had less money. Many walked off farms with nothing. Many shops and businesses closed. Bankruptcies. School starting age raised to 6. The Wall Street Stock market crashed October 1929, key factor in start of the Great

ISBN: 9780170230766

Depression that followed. Helped Labour come to power 1935 as promised to help lift people and country out of six years of misery and suffering caused by depression. Students left school early to work to help family. Massive unemployment. Family breakups. Wages dropped. Queues for soup kitchens. Work relief schemes to provide work but not for females or Maori. 1932 riots in Dunedin, Wellington, Auckland.

Practice 2

Use the notes about the cycle of poverty to write a paragraph about the meaning of cycle of poverty.

Skill: Organising and presenting

- Do a rough copy. Then check it to make sure everything makes sense.
- All you need to write are clear and simple sentences.
- If you have only one short sentence, it shows you have not developed your ideas enough.
- Check you know the meaning of key words; for example **cycle** = a series of events that takes place in an interval of time and then returns again and again unless the cycle is broken.
- Imagine the cycle of poverty as being trapped inside a clothes dryer and being unable to open the door from inside.

Notes about the cycle of poverty: keeps poor locked into being poor, for example, parents of bright child in Somalia might want to send child to school but can't because child has to work to support family; no formal education sets child up for life to get only low-paying jobs, lack of economic choices such as getting loan, feelings of helplessness, lack of money for decent health-care, child's own children also trapped in cycle.

Your paragraph:

_____
_____
_____
_____
_____
_____
_____
_____
_____
_____
_____
_____
_____
_____
_____
_____
_____
_____
_____
_____
_____
_____
_____
_____
_____
_____
_____
_____

ISBN: 9780170230766

Think about identity, culture and organisation: how groups make decisions that impact on communities, and how systems of government in New Zealand operate and affect people's lives.

Being able to identify the main idea and other key words in a paragraph will speed up your research and help you take useful notes. The main idea is the focus, the statement that says what the paragraph is about and other key ideas are the important ideas backing up the main idea. For example, read the following paragraph where the main idea and other key ideas are underlined.

> <u>New Zealand's founding document, the Treaty of Waitangi, was signed on 6 February 1840 at Waitangi in the Bay of Islands between the British Crown and some Maori chiefs.</u> A draft of the Treaty <u>in Maori and English</u> was discussed the day before, in front of about 200 Pakeha and 500 Maori. <u>A few influential chiefs</u> convinced many reluctant chiefs the treaty would be a good thing and next day <u>about 40 signed</u>. The <u>Treaty was then taken around the country</u> for other chiefs to sign and about <u>another 500</u> did so.

Practice 1

Read the text below about democracy in the Ancient Greek city-state of Athens. Then underline or highlight the main idea and other key ideas of each paragraph.

Skill: Close reading and identifying
- Make sure you understand key words; for example, **citizen** = member of a town or city or country, especially one who is allowed to vote; **by lot** = chosen by lottery.
- Read each paragraph carefully to identify the main idea. Ask yourself, What is this paragraph about? Where is the focus?
- Imagine what it would have been like going to a huge open-air meeting in your simple, home-made tunic to decide affairs of state – but only if you were male.

The system of government called democracy developed in the Ancient Greek city-state of Athens about 508 BC. At that time there was no united country of Greece; the area was divided into city-states. With a seaport and a hill for defence, Athens was the largest. Our word politics is from polis, Greek for city-state.

The Greek demos meaning people and kratos meaning power has given us the word democracy although Athenian democracy was different to modern democracy in many ways. For example, New Zealanders today vote for politicians to represent them in Parliament whereas all Athenians who were allowed to vote were also required to attend the Assembly, the equivalent of our Parliament. Another example is that only adult male Athenian citizens who had done military training were allowed to vote and that meant women, foreigners, slaves, and freed slaves had no say in government.

Between ten to forty times a year male citizens who could vote went to the open-air Assembly to vote on actions such as war. Thousands might attend and they voted by a show of hands or by putting coloured pebbles into a jar.

Each year a Council of 500 males was chosen by lot to carry out the decisions of the Assembly. A man could serve on it only once in his life. There were no police but courts tried cases and had juries to get decisions. Every day over 500 jurors were chosen by lot. As there were no rules about what type of cases could be tried and what was said at court, people could use courts to punish their enemies.

Practice 2

Read the text about democracy in New Zealand. Then underline or highlight the main idea of each paragraph.

Skill: Close reading and identifying
- Make sure you understand key words; for example, **neutral** = does not support any political party over another, **chamber** = large room.
- The main idea is not always in the first sentence.
- If you were asked to compare New Zealand's system of government with another you could choose a non-democratic one such as the Nazis in Germany, and communism in China.

New Zealand is a democracy which means its citizens have power over the way they are governed. A much-quoted definition of democracy is US President Abraham Lincoln's - democracy is government of the people for the people by the people.

New Zealand's system of government is based on British tradition. The Queen is New Zealand's head of state and the Governor-General is her appointed representative. They are politically neutral. A bill passed by Parliament becomes law only when one of them has signed it.

Those eligible, most 18-years-olds and over, vote once every three years for members to represent them in Parliament. Voting takes place at special polling booths and you vote behind a screen in private.

Every year the government writes a budget to say how much money it has and where it will spend taxes. The Minister of Finance delivers the budget by making a speech in Parliament. It might include a review of the world economic situation and New Zealand's economy.

Parliament is the only body that can make laws. It consists of a single chamber called the House of Representatives, or The House. It is elected for a maximum three-year term using the Mixed Member Proportional (MMP) system which generally provides 120 Members of Parliament.

If a party wins more than half the seats in Parliament it can become the Government by itself. If no one party has the majority, two or more parties can join together to form a coalition. The Prime Minister is usually the leader of the political party with most seats in Parliament.

The Prime Minister is the head of Cabinet which is the engine-room of Government and meets regularly. It consists of ministers who have special jobs such as the Minister of Youth Development or the Minister of Education.

ISBN: 9780170230766

How to write a diary entry

Think about continuity and change: how events have causes and effects; how ideas and actions of people in the past have had an impact on others' lives.

A **diary** is a set of entries each day about a person's experiences, observations and feelings. One of the most famous books in the world is *The Diary of Anne Frank*. Anne was a Jewish girl who received a diary on her 13th birthday and while she and her family were hiding from Nazis in the Netherlands, she kept up her diary entries. Although the Nazis found Anne's family and Anne died in a concentration camp, the diary survived and made Anne an inspiration to millions of people around the world. If you are asked to write a diary entry where you picture yourself living in a different time or place it is a good way to show how well you have understood what you have been studying.

Practice 1

Use the notes about Germany's surrender at the end of World War 2 to help you write a diary entry of a New Zealander on 9 May 1945.

Skill: Imagining
- Start with the date, usually at the top right corner.
- Write it like a personal email or letter.
- Write about events that happened to you, how you felt and why you felt that way. Use the first person; for example, I, we, us.
- Make it sound as if you are alive at the time; give details about places, people and events.
- Watch out for anachronisms which are mistakes in time; for example, with no mobile phones or internet in 1945 you can not send texts or emails.
- Imagine the mix of emotions you might feel – joy, sadness if a family member or friend had been killed, excitement, relief at knowing soon rationing of food items such as butter and sugar would stop.

VE Day (Victory in Europe) celebrated in New Zealand 9 May 1945, Germany surrendered 7 May but NZ PM told people to wait till 9 May to celebrate. Japan still at war. Sirens, factory hooters, church bells, car horns, whistles, bonfires, costumes, dancing, strangers kissing, school closed, victory caps, flags, shop lights on, hotels ignore laws about closing at 6 o'clock, speeches, bands, parades, sing-songs, victory balls, lines of people, church services.

_____
_____
_____
_____
_____
_____
_____
_____
_____
_____
_____

ISBN: 9780170230766

Practice 2

Use the notes in the box about drought in Kenya to help you write a diary entry as a villager in Kenya during a drought.

Skill: Imagining
- Think how people living in drought get focussed on water, or lack of it.
- Then picture what the physical environment would be like. Some people find it easier to do this when they close their eyes. Then imagine the effect of the environment on peoples' minds.
- One issue is that because of cattle stealing and gun battles people living in areas where food can be grown have been forced to shift to safer areas where food will not grow.
- Imagine how one thing has led to another and so on and so on.

Normally people survive by drinking milk and selling meat of cows and goats but most animals are dead. All men who can walk take few animals still alive to chase reports of rain far away. Food prices sky-high eg. last year one cow got 6 large sacks of rice, now gets 1 small sack. Daughters as young as 13 in arranged marriages to get money from groom's family. Water trucks stopped coming because World Vision ran out of money. Constant hot wind. 40°C heat. Domed huts built of thatch, sticks, rags. Only vegetation is high on trees with poisonous leaves. Village shop bare – no sugar, maize-flour, cooking oil. Children no longer in primary school which used to give them food for attending. Many dead from starvation. Dirt road. Beggars on dusty roadside. Even camels can hardly stand.

ISBN: 9780170230766

31 How to transfer visual information to written information

Think about continuity and change: how events, such as natural disasters, have causes and effects.

When you are asked to transfer **visual information** such as a graph into **written information**, you need to make sure you include all the information from the graph in your paragraph. However, even if you know a lot more about the topic than is included on the graph, you must use only the information on the graph.

Practice 1

Study the graph and answer the questions on it. Then use your answers to write a short paragraph covering the points of the graph.

Skill: Transferring

- Identify the purpose of the graph; for example, to show a pattern of change. Is there a title? Is there a key? Identify details; for example, look for data on the vertical axis and horizontal axis.
- These are weather catastrophes so they do not include earthquakes or tsunamis. Therefore don't mention them in your paragraph.
- You can still use unusual or interesting ways to describe what is happening in the graph. For example, one expert described the trend here as looking as if the weather machine had changed up a gear.
- Make sure you understand key words; for example, **catastrophe** = violent and often destructive natural event, **trend** = general movement or direction, **trend line** = line on a graph made by connecting data points to show a statistical trend.
- Imagine how weather catastrophes are being caused and the effects they are having on people and environment.

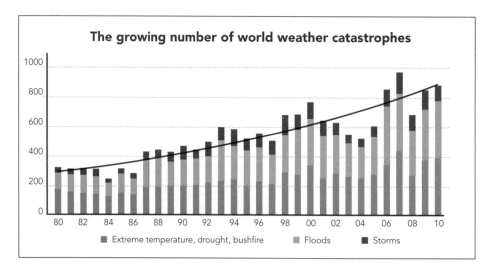

The growing number of world weather catastrophes

Key: ■ Extreme temperature, drought, bushfire ■ Floods ■ Storms

1 What is the topic? _____

2 What is the purpose? _____

3 What are the details? _____

ISBN: 9780170230766

Paragraph: _____

_____

_____

_____

_____

_____

_____

_____

Practice 2

Study the map about aftershocks in Christchurch. Then use your answers to write a short paragraph covering the points of the map.

Skill: Transferring

- Make sure you understand the environment; for example, the Darfield earthquake was 4 September 2010 (also known as Christchurch earthquake), the Christchurch earthquake was 22 February 2011. Darfield is about 35 kms west of Christchurch, aftershocks are quakes that arrive after the main quake.
- Put in the paragraph only what the map shows; for example, it does not show wrecked buildings or trapped people.
- Imagine what it would be like always wondering when the next shock was going to arrive.

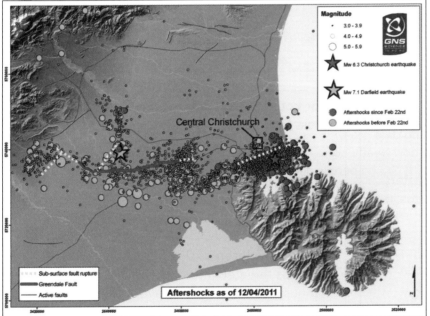

1 What information do the key boxes give?

_____

_____

_____

_____

2 Estimate the best description for the total number of aftershocks; a few or over 50 or over 100 or hundreds and hundreds.

_____

_____

_____

3 Where do most aftershocks seem to be located? _____

_____

Paragraph: _____

_____

_____

_____

_____

_____

_____

_____

ISBN: 9780170230766

How to compare and contrast

Think about the economic world and about identity, culture and organisation: how economic decisions impact on people, communities and nations, and how systems of government operate in NZ and affect people's lives.

Comparing concentrates on similarities, **contrasting** concentrates on differences.

Practice 1

Study the features below about New Zealand and Somalia. Underline features you could compare and contrast. Highlight features you could use if you were to compare and contrast only the economies of the countries.

Skill: Comparing and contrasting

- Look for data on the same features for both countries; for example, population could be a feature because you have populations for both countries but climate could not because you have data on climate for only one.
- Make sure you understand key terms; examples, **urbanisation** = towns and cities, **kWh** = kilowatt hour unit of energy, **cu m** = cubic metre, **bbl** = barrel, **NA** = not applicable (information may not be available), nomads (wander with their animals in search of grazing).
- Think about how your life might be different if you lived in Somalia.

Rich country - New Zealand
- population 4.4 million
- unemployment rate 5.5%
- literacy 99%
- organisations to deal with disasters
- infant mortality rate 4.78 deaths in 1,000 live births
- effective central government
- government pays benefits and pensions
- urbanisation 86% of population
- life expectancy at birth 80.59 years
- electricity production 42.4 billion kWh
- imports $30.24 billion
- exports $33.24 billion
- oil proved reserves 60 million bbl
- natural gas proved reserves 33.98 billion cu m
- GDP per capita $27,700
- no civil war
- high standard of health care
- freedom of speech
- generally safe for visitors
- many rivers and water supplies
- tourism is a big earner

Poor country - Somalia
- less than 0.5 doctors and 2 nurses per 100,000 people
- no effective central government
- unable to deal with famine and disease
- population 9.3 million
- 60% live below the $1 a day poverty line
- unemployment NA
- oil proved reserves 0 bbl
- pirates threaten international shipping
- thousands of refugees leave country
- infant mortality rate 105.56 deaths in 1,000 live births
- life expectancy 50.4 years
- literacy 37.8 %
- GDP per capita $600
- electricity production 280 million kWh
- natural gas proved reserves 5.6 billion cu m
- exports $300 million
- imports $798 million
- urbanisation 37%
- civil war between warlords
- hot all year with winds and irregular rainfall
- much of the population are nomads
- less than 2% of land is suitable for crops

ISBN: 9780170230766

Practice 2

Use the information about New Zealand's systems of government to write four sentences comparing and contrasting four features of national and local government in New Zealand.

New Zealand's national system of government
- deals with issues related to country and people as a nation
- members elected every three years
- people vote for whom they want to represent them in Parliament
- members meet in Parliament in Wellington
- highest ranking officer is Prime Minister
- has Ministers in charge of different areas eg. defence
- makes laws for whole country
- in charge of spending for whole country and collects taxes in whole country to get money.

New Zealand's local system of government
- deals with issues related to local area only
- members elected every three years
- local people vote for whom they want to represent them on councils
- members meet in council buildings in local area
- highest ranking officer is mayor
- different areas have different councils eg. City Councils, District Councils, Auckland Council
- also Regional Councils; for example, Environment Bay of Plenty, which look after the environment and resources of an area
- councils have only the powers given to it by Parliament
- makes bylaws which are laws for just one particular local area
- in charge of spending for just local area and collects rates in local area to get money.

_____
_____
_____
_____
_____
_____
_____
_____
_____
_____
_____
_____

ISBN: 9780170230766

33 Understanding human rights

Think about identity, culture, and organisation: how people define and seek human rights (basic rights and freedoms to which every person in the world is said to be entitled).

An **issue** is a topic or problem that people discuss, debate and try to solve. Examples of issues that affect New Zealand society are the drinking age, global warming, climate change, poverty, and the economy. Opinions about the issue are usually split between those for, and those against. It is easier to have an informed opinion if you read and think about it so you have facts to back you up.

Practice 1

Study the comments below about the issue of New Zealand giving overseas aid, such as money and technical help, to poorer countries. Colour those *for* with one colour and those *against* with another colour.

Skill: Interpreting different points of view
- Arguments *for* something are usually in positive language such as 'helps' whereas arguments *against* something are usually in negative language such as 'does not help'.
- Imagine if you lived in a developing country that depended on aid from countries such as New Zealand for you to get enough food, water and shelter to keep you alive.

New Zealand prides itself on its human rights so it should provide human rights for others.	Developed countries should help developing countries as we are all human.	The world is overpopulated so famine and starvation are nature's way of fixing this problem.	People in poor countries should make their governments look after them instead of spending money on wars.
New Zealand is not rich enough to give money away.	Money might not reach those who need it.	It helps build New Zealand reputation overseas.	It might bring trade benefits for New Zealand.
Aid makes countries dependent on others.	Poverty is too big a problem to solve.	A poor country has only itself to blame.	Rich countries should share their wealth.
Each country should solve its own problems.	There is poverty in New Zealand that should be addressed first.	Giving aid helps make the world politically stable.	Maybe one day New Zealand will need help from a country it helps now.
It shows New Zealand cares about the world.	It is the correct action to take.	New Zealand can afford it.	Many countries don't help so why should we?
We should give aid for education because if every child was educated many of the world's problems would disappear.		People in poor countries may be denied the most basic human rights such as freedom to move in search of food and shelter.	

ISBN: 9780170230766

Practice 2

Study the comments about the issue of whether or not Muslim women in New Zealand should be allowed to wear a burqa, the loose-fitting full-body covering that has a mesh across the eyes so the wearer can see out of it. Then state your opinion on this issue by putting a tick or cross in the Opinion Box and choose ten of the comments you would use to back up your opinion. Show your ten choices by ticking the boxes beside the comments.

Opinion Box:

Personal choice of dress should be respected.	☐
It is a human right to cover your body how you want.	☐

New Zealand was the first country to give females the vote so it should be more accepting.	☐	Muslims in New Zealand may not like non-Muslim dress but they don't get upset about it so why should non-Muslims get upset by Muslim dress?	☐
It can make professionals such as doctors uncomfortable.	☐	Even some Muslims say it has no place in the Muslim religion.	☐
How is it different to other choices of clothing such as a sari or a hoodie?	☐	It can affect health, such as Vitamin D deficiency through not getting enough sun.	☐
New Zealand talks of human rights such as freedom of religion so it should practise what it preaches.	☐	Establishing who you are quickly is sometimes necessary and the burqa makes that impossible.	☐
It is a prison for females.	☐	How is it different to nuns wearing veils?	☐
It is a symbol of men controlling females.	☐	It is a depressing fashion; it is a moving tent.	☐
Weapons can be hidden under it.	☐	It makes it easy to shop-lift.	☐
It saves females from unwelcome male attention.	☐	Those who want to wear it should live in a country where it is common to wear it.	☐
It gives females the freedom to not be judged by how attractive they are.	☐	New Zealand claims to be multicultural so it should embrace all styles of dress.	☐
It is insulting to other people because the wearer cannot communicate with others.	☐	It makes it harder for females to do things such as drive a car.	☐
Men could wear one and hide from police who are looking for them.	☐	It comes in different colours and so it adds variety to fashion on streets.	☐
It helps in New Zealand because wind can blow dust on to your clothes and hair.	☐	Banning it will encourage racists to be more openly anti-Muslim.	☐

ISBN: 9780170230766

Working out perspective

Think about identity, culture and organisation: how nations develop systems of government that affect people's lives.

Many people use the terms perspective, point of view and opinion to mean the same thing although there are differences. **Perspective** means a particular way of seeing based on things such as your job, culture, religion, personality, beliefs, values, age, gender. A famous saying about perspective is 'You don't see things as they are; you see things as you are.' An example of perspective is an artist about to tour Parliament buildings looking at them from a cultural perspective because of the art treasures hanging inside.

Practice 1

Look at the photo. In the boxes below the photo are people who are standing outside the three buildings and looking at them. In the space in each box suggest perspectives the people will see the buildings from. The first has been done as an example.

Skill: Understanding modern perspectives

- Use your background knowledge, for example, Bowen House has offices for many MPs and staff; the Beehive includes the Cabinet room, offices for Cabinet Ministers, restaurants; Parliament House includes the House of Representatives for parliamentary business.
- Ask the question – what do I know about this person that would encourage a particular perspective? For example, a small child might look from a size perspective of how big everything looks.

Architect. *Design of buildings, ability to survive earthquake.*	Gardener.	Prime Minister.
Office-cleaner.	Cabinet minister afraid of heights.	Chef.
Tour guide.	Tagger.	Sacked maintenance worker.

Student with task-sheet on Parliament to do.	Life-long resident of Wellington.	Six-year-old.
Overseas tourist.	Leader of the Opposition.	Security guard.

Practice 2

Look at the painting and caption about the signing of the Treaty of Waitangi on February 6 1840. Choose one person who was present (it can be a key person such as Hobson or an unnamed person such as a British settler) and write a few sentences about the person's perspective on the treaty.

Skill: Understanding historical perspectives

- Ask the question – what fact/s do I know about this person that would encourage a particular perspective? For example, a grog-seller from Korareka (Russell), described as the hell-hole of the Pacific, will look at the treaty from the perspective that it could damage his business by bringing in British officials to get law and order and introduce rules and regulations he will be forced to obey.
- Use any background knowledge, for example, in 1840 more Maori than British lived in New Zealand and technology was more basic – no computers, no cars, no electricity …

The chief signing the treaty is Tamati Waka Nene, Nga Puhi leader and trader, who wanted order and believed Lieutenant Governor Hobson would be like a father and peacemaker. Among the British officials present were William Hobson of the British Royal Navy, who arrived in New Zealand on January 29 with instructions to set up a British colony, and James Busby, sent by Britain to be British Resident in New Zealand in 1833 to protect British settlers and traders, and stop European outrages against Maori. Also present were missionary Henry Williams who believed Maori should be protected against European lawlessness and dodgy land deals, and William Colenso, the Church Mission printer. Other people included British settlers and traders, James Freeman who was Hobson's secretary, and other Maori chiefs, some of whom were against signing.

_____

_____

_____

_____

_____

_____

_____

_____

_____

_____

_____

_____

ISBN: 9780170230766

Index and Skills summary

ISBN: 9780170230766